Totally Teen With Print

SCRAPBOOK PAGES

Maybe it's the memories of Fear Factor night at his house, maybe it's the fact that he's had almost as many injuries as I've had over the years, could be because he loves volleyball, maybe we are just more alike than different – I'm not really sure what it is, but there is something that connects me with this kid. Yes, he's my nephew and therefore, we are connected by blood. But that's only part of it. Yes, we are always kidding around, playing jokes on one another and trying to "one-up" each other – but I don't think that's all there is to it either. The connection goes deeper than that. It's a heart-to-heart connection that draws me to want to see the man he will become and to enjoy each opportunity I have to spend time with him. He really is a very special kid!

Brett

Scrapbooking the Almost Grown-Up Years

MEMORY MAKERS BOOKS

Editors of Memory Makers Books, Denver, Colorado

Managing Editor MaryJo Regier

Editor Amy Glander

Art Director Nick Nyffeler

Graphic Designers Jordan Kinney, Robin Rozum

Art Acquisitions Editor Janetta Abucejo Wieneke

Craft Editor Jodi Amidei

Photographer Ken Trujillo

Contributing Photographers Lizzy Creazzo, Jennifer Reeves

Contributing Writer Pennie Stutzman

Editorial Support Karen Cain, Kari Hansen, Emily Curry Hitchingham, Dena Twinem

Contributing Memory Makers Masters Jessie Baldwin, Valerie Barton, Kathy Fesmire, Angie Head, Nic Howard, Kelli Noto, Suzy Plantamura, Torrey Scott, Denise Tucker, Sharon Whitehead

Hair & Makeup Artist Trisha McCarty-Luedke

Memory Makers ® *Totally Teen Scrapbook Pages*
Copyright © 2006
All rights reserved.

Published by Memory Makers Books, an imprint of F+W Publications, Inc.
12365 Huron Street, Suite 500, Denver, CO 80234
Phone (800) 254-9124
First edition. Printed in the United States.
10 09 08 07 06 5 4 3 2 1

Library of Congress Cataloging-in-Publication Data

Totally teen scrapbook pages : scrapbooking the almost grown-up years.
     p. cm.
   Includes index.
   ISBN-13: 978-1-892127-74-7
   ISBN-10: 1-892127-74-1
     1. Photograph albums. 2. Photographs--Conservation and restoration. 3. Scrapbooks. 4. Teenagers--Collectibles. I. Memory Makers Books.

TR465.T68 2005
745.593--dc22

                                                                          2005054405

Distributed to trade and art markets by
F+W Publications, Inc.
4700 East Galbraith Road, Cincinnati, OH 45236
Phone (800) 289-0963

Distributed in Canada by
Fraser Direct
100 Armstrong Avenue
Georgetown, ON, Canada L7G 5S4
Tel: (905) 877-4411

Distributed in the U.K. and Europe by
David & Charles
Brunel House, Newton Abbot,
Devon, TQ12 4PU, England
Tel: (+44) 1626 323200,
Fax: (+44) 1626 323319
E-mail: mail@davidandcharles.co.uk

Distributed in Australia by Capricorn Link
P.O. Box 704, S. Windsor NSW, 2756 Australia
Tel: (02) 4577-3555

Memory Makers Books is the home of *Memory Makers*, the scrapbook magazine dedicated to educating and inspiring scrapbookers. To subscribe, or for more information, call (800) 366-6465.
Visit us on the Internet at www.memorymakersmagazine.com

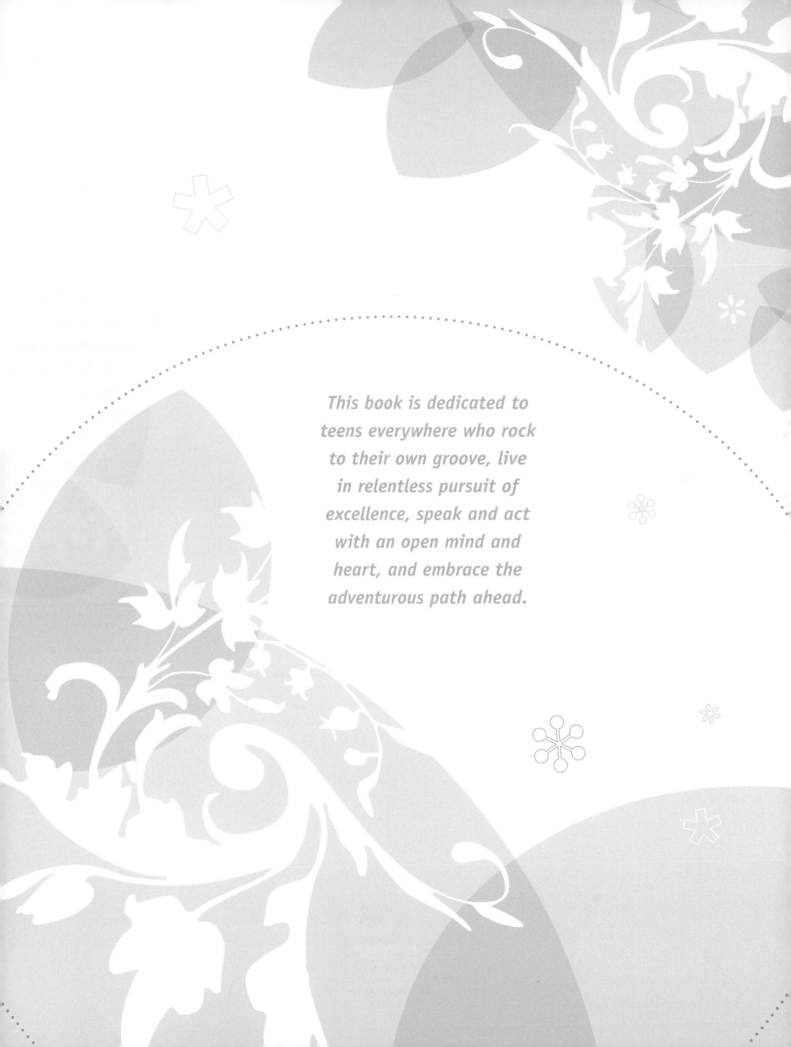

This book is dedicated to teens everywhere who rock to their own groove, live in relentless pursuit of excellence, speak and act with an open mind and heart, and embrace the adventurous path ahead.

Table of Contents

CHAPTER ONE

Times Like These • 10

Celebrate your teen's accomplishments, milestones and special occasions through stunning pages that commemorate each precious moment.

CHAPTER TWO

All You Need Is Love • 32

Love is what makes the world go round so what better way to chronicle your teen's special connections to friends, family, high school sweethearts and others than through pages that warm the heart and touch the soul.

CHAPTER THREE

Livin' the Good Life • 54

Live it up through action-infused scrapbook pages that document the activities, hobbies, interests and favorites of your live-in-the-moment teen.

CHAPTER FOUR

What I Like About You • 84

What special qualities make your teen truly his or her own person? Document the unique traits and characteristics of your one-of-a-kind youngster on pages all about him or her.

Introduction

"Those who dance are considered insane by those who cannot hear the music."
–George Carlin

The teen years sure are hard to decode. I remember working hard to balance school with friends, figuring out how to get along with my parents, crushing over cute boys in my classes and uncovering the person I knew I someday wanted to become. I realized I had to find my own true calling, allow myself to be creative, seek new outlets for self-expression and discipline myself to set challenges and work hard to achieve them. The person I found was the one and only me. Only time and experience could have taught me that the journey is just as important as the destination.

Teens keep it real. They roll with the punches, hang out with the crew, rock a look that is all their own and embrace life with all its possibilities. *Totally Teen Scrapbook Pages: Scrapbooking the Almost Grown-Up Years* will take you on a tour of teen planet complete with tips for how to fashion teen scrapbook pages reflective of the special teen in your life. This book offers a gallery of pages showcasing the fun, funky, edgy, fashion-inspired side of teens. What infuses them? What are their passions? What sets their hearts afire? Is she glamorous, sporty or the girl next door? Is he rebellious, retro, a natural-born leader or the world's next all-star? You'll find all this and more, including twelve informative sidebars offering useful information on photography, memorabilia, journaling and more.

At long last, here's your scrapbook owner's manual for documenting the life and times of your teen. With insights into what teens love, how they spend their time and who they spend their time with, this book will get you to look a little deeper and see life once again through the wide-eyed world of an individual about to embark on the journey of life. So fasten your seat belt and get ready for a wild ride to Teen Street where the exhilaration and discovery will keep you alive in the moment and reliving the precious memories of teen years past.

Amy

Amy Glander

Associate Editor

SAM

AMIDEI'S 09/05
B-DAY PARTY,
FOR JIMI AND MIKE
COUSINS ALL ROCKIN'
AND ROLLIN'

¡bada bing!

SAMANTHA - 16

JAMMIN'

PRETTY N' TRENDY

Discover products that will adorn photos of your prettiest girly girl. Patterned papers in soft pastels, sparkly beads and feminine clips will make your pages simmer with fashionista flair!

PLAYERS OF THE YEAR

There's no better way to showcase a teen champ than with this rough and tough collection of sports-related products. Epoxy word stickers and metal accents resembling varsity medals shout true team spirit.

HEAD OF THE CLASS

Get extra credit with these exciting school-related products. Woven labels, photo corners and letter stickers provide scholastic style that's sure to earn you an A+!

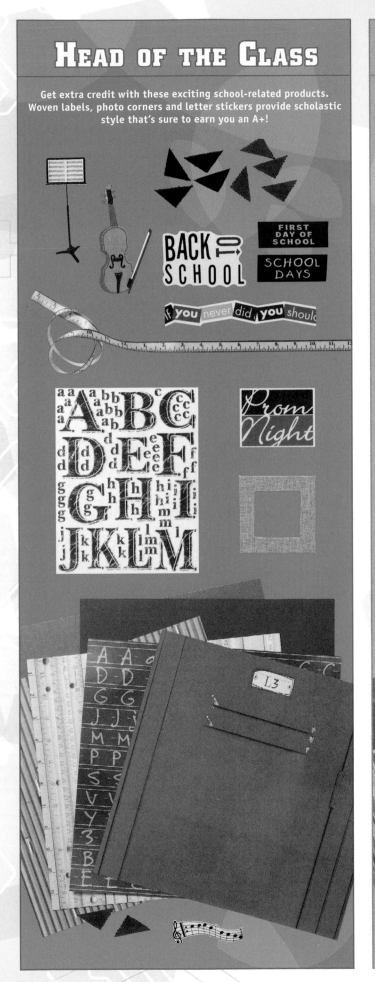

IT'S A GUY THING

Boys will boys and there's no better way to feature their masculine personalites than with urban-style papers, border stickers and rubber tire tracks that speak true macho charm.

Times Like These

KATIE

TRACY

IN FULL BLOOM

After twelve years of watering and nurturing care, these two exquisite flowers are now in full bloom…ready to let the world see their beauty, gifts, and skills.

K BELIEVE T

EXPLORE GOOD

JOY

LIVE LOVE

Oh, the places you'll go...the wise words of Dr. Seuss so perfectly encapsulate the journey of adolescence. The teen years are filled with typical school days hanging out between classes, birthday bashes with best buds, getting glammed up for prom and announcing to the world "I Made It" by graduating with true teen flair. These milestones not only mark the high points of teen life but are perfect opportunities to snap your teen at his or her best. So whether your photo subject is an academic whiz kid, a foxy fella, an ultra-chic cosmo girl or an adventure-seeker out to take on the world, they're sure to make a stunning entrance on your scrapbook pages.

Between classes . . . there is always time to chat, find a friend, share a story, exchange notes. It is the gathering place, where secrets shared of a new crush, an old disappointment, a certain triumph whisper through the shaded halls. The place between history and math, P.E. and art, French and English. A moment to rest, relax, gather strength for the next hour of education. Backpacks litter the ground, and conversations mix and mingle and drift away, and all is well with the world.

2005

Confident Women

At any school, any day, the little slice of time between classes is the foundation of student connections, and Jennifer's insightful journaling brings these moments to life. Inspired by the uniform colors, Jennifer's design features playful paper stitching, a carefree button border and a monogram with the school initial.

Jennifer S. Gallacher, Savannah, Georgia

Supplies: Patterned papers (All My Memories, Chatterbox); heart button (Doodlebug Design); shape buttons, embroidery floss, eyelet snaps (Making Memories); letter and number rub-ons, chipboard letter (Li'l Davis Designs); acrylic expression (KI Memories); circle printing (Microsoft WordArt); ribbon (Offray); photo corners (Canson); corner rounder (McGill); textured cardstock (Bazzill); circle cutter

Half Time

Until the band comes out and Alex conducts, Kathy is oblivious to what happens on the field. Kathy anchors her horizontal format with a large photo of drum major Alex, and then inserts a sophisticated tone into her design by contrasting bright feminine embellishments with a toneless and textured background.

Kathy Fesmire, Athens, Tennessee

Photo: Reneé Nicolo of Home Run Photography, Englewood, Tennessee

Supplies: Patterned papers (Kangaroo & Joey, Provo Craft); letter stickers (American Crafts, Mustard Moon); mesh (Magic Mesh); metal-rimmed tag (Making Memories); label maker (Dymo); letter stencil (Plaid); ribbons (Making Memories, Offray); staples; stamping ink; cardstock

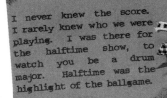

I never knew the score. I rarely knew who we were playing. I was there for the halftime show, to watch you be a drum major. Halftime was the highlight of the ballgame.

fUn DISCOVERY

SCHOOL

Admit it.... Not every school trip to a science museum is a teen's idea of fun! This trip was totally different though! Bethany, Brittany and Breanna were hooked the minute they walked into Ft. Discovery. Hundreds of flashy "try me out" interactive displays covered two whole floors. The girls spent all day hopping from one display to another (and learning the whole time!) Bethany was the first one on the real motorcycle (main photo.) The other girls soon followed suit. The resistance luge (#1) was pretty cool too. Bethany just had to try this one on for size! The dinosaur display was life-sized and almost scary (#2.) The museum even had a gyroscope (#3) in which you could move your whole body in multiple spins in any direction by shifting your weight around. Breanna spent a lot of time flipping herself around on it. The telephone display (#4) was really cool. There was an actual switchboard that you could control and connect different phones to each other. Yep, telephones...just what three teen girls need for a good time! All the way home my girls couldn't stop talking about the field trip. It was definitely one of the best museums they had ever been too and they couldn't wait to go back. (If they only knew how much they had really discovered that day! Shh!)   Ft. Discovery, Augusta, Georgia

① ② ③ ④

Fun Discovery School

The happy enthusiasm of these photos reminded Sharon how quickly the science museum's flashy fun turned her daughters' boring field trip into a cool encounter with learning. Sharon playfully creates a technological look in her layout by placing wire mesh and metal accents onto a grid format.

Sharon Laakkonen, Superior, Wisconsin

Supplies: Stencil letters, wire mesh (Making Memories); wooden numbers (Li'l Davis Designs); metal letters (DieCuts with a View); letter brads, square brads, ribbon (Queen & Co.); textured cardstock (Bazzill); brads; acrylic paint

TEEN LINGO

Looking to translate teen speak into creative titles or journaling for your layouts? Teens have a vernacular all their own and it only makes sense that you'd want to reflect their witty commentary on your pages. Here's a list of popular words and phrases that will get you well-versed in their vogue vocabulary.

2 cool 4 school	fab flirting	it girl/boy!	style on trial
A+ for style	fashion crave	it's all about…	super smarty
all dolled up	fashion patrol	just 4 you	teen 2 teen
all glammed up	fave	keepin' it real	teen spirit
carefree	first impressions	kickin' back	teens decoded
casual cool	fun n' games	killer smile	that rules!
celebrate	fun peeps to hang with	latest and greatest	the real deal
check it out!	funky fashion	latest craze	the scoop
chica	gab for hours	leaders of the pack	time to shine
circle of friends	get glammed	let it roll	totally in tune
class act	get groovin'	loosen up and have some fun	trend alert
class smarty	giggle	mi vida loca	true confessions
commemorate	girl/boy power	outfitted	ultimate
cosmically cool	good times	outrageous	ultra-chic
cosmo girl	good, clean fun	perfect pals	unique style
dance-off	groovy	playful	wear it with pride, baby!
deal of the day	hangin' out with the crew	retro revival	what a teen wants
denim mania	highlight your life	rock star	wild style
drama queen	honor	rockin' a look	you got the vibe?
dynamic duos	how to deal	roll the dice and make your move	you in?
edgy	ignite	s/he's got game	your life
embrace the future	inside scoop	so last season	you've got the look

13

Realizing that Emma was now official-
ly a teen, Kathy created a layout that
honors the inspirations and experiences of her daughter's life to date.
To construct the numbers, Kathy used
bright funky paper combined with a
photo montage to create a collage of
special moments.

*Kathy Thompson Laffoley, Riverview,
New Brunswick, Canada*

Supplies: Patterned paper (KI Memories); textured
cardstock (Bazzill); circle punch

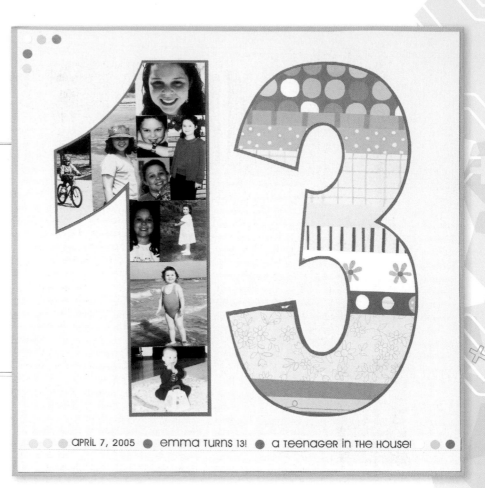

APRIL 7, 2005 ● emma TURNS 13! ● a TEENAGER IN THE HOUSE!

celebrate

Celebrate this day
and embrace all
the reasons to believe
in wishes again.
-Flavia

Kristen
2004

Celebrate

It was the colors of her niece's birthday photo
that inspired Miki to create this delightful
layout full of funky fun. With geometrics to
keep things hip and trendy, Miki's layout subtly
reinforces the celebration theme with stamped
images on paper circles and poly shrink charms.

Miki Benedict for Paper Salon, Modesto, California

Photo: Tim Benedict, Manteca, California

Supplies: Patterned papers, birthday stamps (Paper Salon); slide
mount (Design Originals); expression die cuts (Colorbök); epoxy letters (Creative Imaginations); poly shrink paper (Lucky Squirrel); ribbon (Offray); circle cutter (Creative Memories); tag; colored pencils

So You're 15

Jordon celebrated her 15th birthday with friends and shopping, the essence of a teen girl's life. Angie's punchy layout reflects the day's lighthearted fun and, by using wallet-size photos plus a journaling door that doubles as a pocket, her design fits an ingenious amount of material onto the page.

Angie Head, Friendswood, Texas

Photos: Tammy Null, Olathe, Kansas

Supplies: Patterned papers (Junkitz); film strip transparency (Creative Imaginations); traced die-cut numbers (source unknown); traced chipboard letters (Li'l Davis Designs); rub-on letters, hinges, flower brad (Making Memories); silk flowers; ribbon; stamping ink; pen

What does a girl who is celebrating her 15th birthday most want to do?
... Shop ...
Gone are the days of party hats (well...) birthday cakes with candles and party favors. Now it is all about gathering a few good friends & heading out for the mall. Happy 15th Birthday Jordan !!!

SWEET

Danielle years ago I would see you and would try to imagine what you would be like as a teenager and I thought that day would never come. Well not only are you a teenager now but somehow you have already turned 16, where has all this time gone too. Looking back at these pictures I can see how totally blessed you are not only with family but also friends that really do love and care about you. Danielle you are truly a beautiful young lady and I hope that all your dreams and wishes do come true. Love you, Aunt Donna
September 25, 2004

16

Sweet 16

Once Donna dreamed about Danielle becoming a teenager; now she wonders where the time went. This energetic design plays pattern against pattern finally chasing our eyes toward the tranquility of the photo block. To insert some fanciful depth to her layout, Donna built painted and glazed flower accents.

Donna Garza, Romeoville, Illinois

Supplies: Patterned papers (Paper Fever); letter stickers (source unknown); flower punch (EK Success); chipboard numbers, buttons, brads (Making Memories); textured cardstock (Bazzill); crystal lacquer (Sakura Hobby Craft); ribbon (May Arts); acrylic paint

16

Cake

Knowing that emerging adults are still part child, Sandra's birthday wish for her daughter was to never grow too old for fun and bear hugging. Sandra's layout is also built with whimsical fun inspired by the spots and colors of the ladybug cake.

Sandra Blazek, Franksville, Wisconsin

Supplies: Rub-on sentiments (Royal & Langnickel): rub-on numbers (Provo Craft); textured cardstock (Bazzill); ribbon (Michaels); bear punch (Hobby Lobby); corner rounder, circle punches (Creative Memories); brads (Karen Foster Design)

You're never too old for a new teddy bear and a cute birthday cake.

It's hard to believe you're 17, it seems like you were just a little girl with pig tails, tights and carrying a stuffed animal.

Through the years you've had some fun cakes. This was one of my favorites. I liked it so much I ordered the same cake for Carli's birthday a month later.

It's hard to imagine in less than a year you will be an adult! My wish for you is that you always remember to enjoy life and you're never to old to give a teddy bear a hug!!

18 Candles

Eye-catching it may be, but Sharon created this lovely layout as a place to record her own feelings as she watched her child come of age. Sharon's design uses minimal stitched and floral accents to keep the layout's focus on her large and beautiful photo.

Sharon Laakkonen, Superior, Wisconsin

Supplies: Patterned papers, cut-out letters (FontWerks); epoxy letter (Creative Imaginations); number stickers (SEI); textured cardstock (Bazzill); ribbon (Making Memories); lace; transparency; silk flower

Payday

It begins with her son's proud smile as he stands before a mall, first paycheck in hand. Next comes the shoe inset, then the pocketed sales receipt, and a happy ending prevails. Mandy's delightful tale unfolds in this layout which she unified with a circle theme throughout.

Mandy McQuillis, Port Vue, Pennsylvania

Supplies: Patterned paper (Basic Grey); letter stamps (PSX Design); letter stickers (American Crafts); ribbon, fiber (Great Balls of Fiber); photo anchors, spiral clip, staples (Making Memories); tag (Daisy D's); textured cardstock (Bazzill); distress ink (Ranger); brads; circle punches

1 Hot Lifegaurd

Teri has such a bright personality that Heidi ignored cool pool ideas and went straight to sizzling in this proud layout about her conscientious sister. While Heidi's floral theme keeps the page feminine, her design uses a stitched border and daisy accent to draw your eye to the focal photo on this computer-generated layout.

Heidi Dillon, Salt Lake City, Utah

Supplies: Patterned papers, round letters, tab, square brads (Shabby Citrus kit by Shabby Princess, www.theshabbyshoppe.com); epoxy number (Kiss the Sun kit by Traci Sims, www.scrapbook-elements.com); rectangle letters (Oh Happy Day kit by Heather Ann Melzer, www.heateranndesigns.com); flower (Sunny Side Up kit by Jen Wilson, www.scrapbookbytes.com); stitching (Sun Room Straight Stitches by Holly McCaig, www.thedigichick.com); staple (Dirt Boy kit by Shabby Princess, www.theshabbyshoppe.com)

Stephanie picked out her 1st REAL job when she was 7. That was the year her brother became a lifeguard & she joined the swim team. When she was 10, her sister also joined the ranks of the ELITE - the lifeguards. Stephanie became a pool rat, hanging around after lessons and swim team practice. BIG STEP at age 13 - Jr. Lifeguard! This meant helping with lessons and being the victim during rescues. FINALLY two weeks before her 15th birthday, she signed up for Lifeguard training. She PASSED all the tests and was offered a job. After 8 years of determination and planning ahead, it was official. Stephanie was a REAL LIFEGUARD!

Journey to a Job

Revealing both the dedicated employee at work and the girly girl who accessorizes a wet look, these photos capture the essence of Stephanie at 15. Patterns and acrylic texture give Karen's layout a poolside sense, and for documentation she incorporates tiny copies of Stephanie's hard-earned certifications.

Karen Cain, Memory Makers Books

Photos: Emily Hare, Denver, Colorado

Supplies: Patterned papers (Arctic Frog); acrylic letters (Junkitz); cardstock

MEMORABILIA

It's likely you've saved precious mementos that mark a special event or occasion in your teen's life. These mementos, also known as memorabilia, can be items saved from school, field trips, travel, sporting events, etc., and can include letters, clippings, postcards, souvenirs or anything that helps you remember that special time. You can copy on a high-quality color copier or scan items and scale down to miniature or, if they are small enough, include them directly onto your layouts. Here's a list of fun ideas for teen-related memorabilia:

- awards or certificates
- medals, ribbons or varsity letter
- middle school or high school diploma
- prom, sporting event, graduation tickets
- newspaper clippings
- driver's permit or license
- first paycheck
- report card or class schedule
- bulletin or program from school play, sporting event or graduation
- favorite clothing labels
- birthday or graduation cards

- hair ribbons (in school colors or teen's favorite colors)
- flyers, brochures or postcards from class field trips (whether close to home or abroad)
- letters of recommendation or words of wisdom from favorite teachers
- clippings from diaries, journals, love letters or notes passed in class (assuming your teen has given you permission of course!)
- CD or DVD jackets from favorite musicians and movies
- concert or movie tickets
- fabric ur swatches from prom or graduation attire or favorite pair of jeans (assuming your teen will no longer don the treasured garb)

Megan bought her car even before she could drive, she was that anxious! She brought her contour home at the end of September (she pd. cash for it w/ her own money!) & got her permit dec. 1st. she drove ALL day! . 12/04

cAR fActs
.automatic . 4 door
.cd player
*98 ford contour SPORT

New Car & Driver

Having purchased her car months before, Megan finally gained the right to use the key. To document her sister's elation at that long-awaited moment, Nichole's layout combines inked papers, a hip circle and brad embellishment, and several sassy letter styles into a fresh, contemporary design.

Nichole Winstead, Smithville, Ohio

Supplies: Patterned papers (KI Memories, Lasting Impressions); letter stickers (Chatterbox, Doodlebug Design); rub-on letters (Making Memories); circle and flower punches (EK Success); textured cardstock (Bazzill); stamping ink; brads

Brand New Car

Traveling from surprise to excitement, Amy's daughter arrived at wild joy before her odometer left zero. Likewise, Amy's layout explodes with dramatic energy through her use of multiple textures, funky colors, and firework effect of her patterned paper.

Amy Goldstein for Junkitz, Kent Lakes, New York

Supplies: Patterned paper, metal ring, metal frame, rubber expression (Junkitz); patterned paper, epoxy letters and circles (MOD-my own design); rub-on letters (Making Memories); brads

When you turned 17, you had your first car accident, and, although it wasn't your fault, we felt an older model car was in order until your driving skills were a little more **REFINED**. So you were driving an old car with 200,000 miles on the odometer. Well eventually, you assuaged our fears and showed us the responsibility needed and we surprised you with your first new car. The look on your face was sheer JOY.

Oh, the wild joys of living

Brand new Car

Why I Admire You

After facing down leukemia at 7, Rebecca thinks she looks at life differently from other 13-year-olds; Lora created this striking layout to proudly agree with her courageous niece. In her layout, Lora increases the smaller photo's presence with a pocket, thereby balancing the weight of her photos.

Lora Covington, Superior, Colorado

Supplies: Patterned paper, metal frame (K & Company); pocket (Chatterbox); metal flower (All My Memories); rub-on expressions (Doodlebug Design); label holder (Making Memories); ribbon; clear transparency

When I was three months pregnant with my first son Abe, my niece Rebecca was diagnosed with Leukemia. She was 7 years old. As I watched Rebecca go through her treatments I wondered why someone so young, beautiful and innocent had to deal with such an experience. There were times she was so sick we didn't know if she would make it. It was a hard time for her. She missed a whole year from school, lost some of her friendships and grew up in a way that you shouldn't have to at such a young age. And through this whole time she accepted her life as it was. She talked about what she wanted to do and be when she was better. She was positive and full of life even though sometimes her medication made her cranky. After two years, Rebecca was cancer free and she is now very healthy and happy. About a year ago, we were driving together and she said to me that she is a stronger person because of what she experienced. She felt that she was a different person, someone who looks at life a little differently than the average 13 year old. I wish Rebecca hadn't gone through such an experience but I admire her for her perseverance, her courage and her stamina. She has taught me to appreciate the little things with my two sons and everyday I am grateful they are healthy and happy.

It's a Big World!

Most children grow worldlier as they mature, but Eric went to extremes, progressively qualifying for geographic bees all the way to the national level. To emphasize modern geography as her layout theme, Kelli used an atlas page under epoxy blocks and as a frame wrapping. Small black accents insert additional interest.

Kelli Noto, Centennial, Colorado

Supplies: Die-cut letters and globe (QuickKutz); epoxy squares (Creative Imaginations); stamping ink; cardstock

When Eric came home from school with a letter saying that he had qualified for the school Geographic Bee Finals, we were surprised. He was struggling with seventh-grade social studies because he wasn't enjoying it. What do they study in seventh-grade social studies? GEOGRAPHY! We went to watch Eric at his school and were thrilled when he won handily. The questions were tough and John and I didn't even know half of them. Eric took a written test to qualify for the State Geographic Bee. They would invite only the top one hundred scorers for the National Geographic Bee. He got the needed score. There was a month of study before the State Bee. Eric surrounded himself with maps and books to prepare as best he could. The world is such a big place though with no way to learn it all. The oral rounds of the State Bee had questions that left the teachers in the auditorium scratching their heads and a couple of the questions tripped up Eric as well. Eric went home without the half scholarship to DU or the trip to Washington, D.C. for the National Finals. Nevertheless, it was still a wonderful experience and that kid now knows more about the world than I ever will.

Emily's Not Out To...

Some feats deserve a good brag, and Vanessa just couldn't hold back about Emily's. In fact, she had so many achievements to record, Vanessa feared they might take over the layout. To keep them in control, Vanessa enlarged her focal photo, kept her embellishments minimal, and let Emily's accomplishments do the rest.

Vanessa Spady, Virginia Beach, Virginia

Photos: Susan Goffman, Gainesville, Florida

Supplies: Fabric papers (Michael Miller Memories); cardstock

Emily's Not Out To Conquer The World...
[just Florida].

Academic:

9th and 10th Grade Honor Roll

Pre-International Baccalaureate Program

Student of the Month

Service:

Volunteer for Children's Miracle Network

Chain Reaction Youth Leadership

Council for the March of Dimes, Health Conference Chair, 2005-2006

Drama:

Amadeus (Actress)
Once Upon This Island and Midsummer Night's Dream (Costume Designer)

Into the Woods (piano)

Superior Rating at State Thespian Conference

Outstanding Achievement in Drama

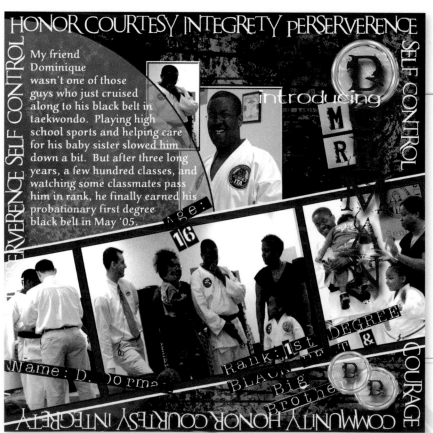

My friend Dominique wasn't one of those guys who just cruised along to his black belt in taekwondo. Playing high school sports and helping care for his baby sister slowed him down a bit. But after three long years, a few hundred classes, and watching some classmates pass him in rank, he finally earned his probationary first degree black belt in May '05.

Introducing
Mr. Dorman

This ceremony honored Dominique's new rank and his perseverance. As an active teen, he balanced school, sports and sister care with earning his tae kwon do black belt. In her computer-generated layout, Barb maneuvers her photos and fonts to resemble a video news bulletin and creates depth with layering and shadows.

Barb Hogan, Cincinnati, Ohio

Supplies: Image-editing software (Adobe Photoshop Elements); patterned paper (Kim Crothers, www.scrapbookbytes.com); metal letters (Emily Boesch); circle tags, frames (source unknown)

size

growth

spurT

6 INCHES THIS YEAR

Up Up and Away

Some people ask what we've been feeding you. Nothing magic, after all, most 13 year olds grow. This just happened to be the year you decided to break the charts ⟶ Go Mason!

Growth Spurt

Speaking of big achievements, Mason grew so much in a year that Deb barely kept pace with his sizes. To record his huge "feat" in this larger than life computer-generated layout, Deb photographed Mason from an ant's-eye view and included oversized, cropped examples of his immense accomplishment.

Deb Perry, Newport News, Virginia

Supplies: Image-editing software (Adobe Photoshop Creative Suite 2.0); circle and green frames (Abstract Art kit by Denise Docherty, www.digitalamour.com); brown frame (Pea Blossom kit by Rhonna Farrer, www.twopeasinabucket.com); digital pencil (Wacom Tablet)

PROPORTION
A fun way to add visual creativity to a layout is to experiment with the proportion of one element in opposition to the others. By enlarging a photo of an object in size in relation to the whole, it becomes the focal point and draws the reader's attention. This can be an effective technique if executed correctly. Be sure that the remaining photos, accents or other elements are not overpowered by the larger element. For more information on using proportion and scale to enhance visual appeal, reference "Proportion and Scale" by Kari Hansen (pages 46–48) in the October 2005 issue of *Memory Makers* magazine.

Winter Ball

The inspiration for this romantic page came from the chic photo of Dianne's daughter and her date. Dianne's layout intermingles genteel trim and embossed roses with tuxes and contemporary hardware to produce a sophisticated and elegant his-and-her design.

Dianne Hudson for Creative Imaginations, Tulsa, Oklahoma

Supplies: Patterned papers, printed transparency, rub-on letters and expressions (Creative Imaginations); rub-on expression (Making Memories); stamp expressions (Hero Arts, Wordsworth); metal links, buckle (7 Gypsies); ribbon numbers (Me & My Big Ideas); printed twill (source unknown); trim; ribbon; acrylic paint; fabric; dried flowers; ultra thick embossing powder; staples

Beautiful Girl

Having moved just prior to prom, Jordan accompanied a casual acquaintance to the dance. With the date being a small factor to the evening, Suzy focused her layout on Jordan's elegant appearance. The piano photo centers Suzy's layout design, and she covers transparencies with rub-ons to create her own sophisticated accents.

Suzy Plantamura, Laguna Niguel, California

Supplies: Patterned paper (Autumn Leaves); pattern and embossed paper (Paper Adventures); printed transparencies, rub-on letters (Creative Imaginations); frame and diamond rub-ons (Heidi Swapp); rubber frame (Scrapworks); metal corners (source unknown); vellum; stamping ink

Prom Checklist

It takes a list to be prepared, and Heidi's catalog of her little sister's preparations confirms that Teri was totally ready for a fabulous time. The clean and uncluttered elegance of Heidi's computer-generated layout gives the playful photos total control, and her tongue-in-cheek presentation expresses the bright fun of the occasion.

Heidi Dillon, Salt Lake City, Utah

Supplies: Patterned papers, ribbons, die-cut journaling (www.scrapbook-elements.com); photo anchors (Cosmo Chick kit by Michelle Underwood, www.scrapbook-elements.com); letters (Rhonna Farrer, www.twopeasinabucket.com); vellum (artist's own design)

Prom

A dog in a prom shot? It's unusual, but Valerie planned this layout to suit Rachael's preferences. Impressed by the brilliant colors of Rachael's corsage, Valerie infused her layout with the small vibrant hues, working them into both her block design and the silk flower embellishments.

Valerie Barton, Flowood, Mississippi

Supplies: Embossed stickers (EK Success); letter stamps (FontWerks); rub-on letters (Autumn Leaves); flower brads (Doodlebug Design); buttons (Magic Scraps); cardstock; silk flowers; vellum

Senior Prom was quite an event! Rachael was escorted by her good friend Chris Fidler. Her beautiful dress was made with love by Mom. They began the evening with dinner at O'Charley's before heading to the Crowne Plaza in Springfield.

A Dance Without Dates?

The absence of boys in these photos made Angie ponder until her own eighth-grade memories returned and she recalled how girls go with friends but boogie with lots of guys. For this decidedly feminine layout, Angie cut expressions from paper and built a journaling folder from a double-sided print.

Angie Head, Friendswood, Texas

Photos: Tammy Null, Olathe, Kansas

Supplies: Patterned papers (American Traditional Designs, SEI); traced die-cut letters (Basic Grey); traced sticker letters (American Crafts); letter stickers, rub-on flower (C-Thru Ruler); file folder template (Provo Craft); textured cardstock (Bazzill); ribbons (Doodlebug Design, May Arts, www.ribbongirls.com); brads; silk flowers

Homecoming

Taking her cue from the dresses, Kay created a striking layout for these photos of her daughter and her friend preparing for a formal dance. Kay's design contrasts chic paper with quirky textures for a feeling of young elegance, and her mini book provides more journaling and photo space.

Kay Rogers, Midland, Michigan

Supplies: Patterned papers (Anna Griffin, Autumn Leaves); leather flowers, rub-on expressions, metal-rimmed tag, woven label, ribbon, mini brads (Making Memories); epoxy expressions, slide mounts, printed transparency (Creative Imaginations); photo anchors, epoxy stickers (Autumn Leaves); distress ink (Ranger)

Graduation

Life is my college. May I graduate well, and earn some honors!

-Louisa May Alcott

com·mence·ment: n. 1. A beginning; a start. 2. A ceremony at which academic degrees or diplomas are conferred. 3. The day on which such a ceremony occurs.

I did it!

The things taught in schools and ... but the means of education. - F...

Graduation

Wanting a distinctive exhibit for her son Carlos' senior portraits, Maripi created this elegant layout. Inspired by the formality and tones of the photos, Maripi's black-tie design also includes small lively accents to draw your eye to the focal photo and add some fun.

Maripi Aldanese, Foster City, California

Photos: Prestige Portraits by Lifetouch, Redwood City, California

Supplies: Patterned paper (Basic Grey); themed stickers (EK Success); spiral stamp (Hero Arts); number stamps (Creative Imaginations); letter stickers (Me & My Big Ideas); printed transparency (Karen Foster Design); acrylic paint

The Grad

Kay's exotic layout is both a tribute to her daughter's graduation and a record of how proud she is of Emily's accomplishments. Inspired by the photo background and the tropical paper, Kay's design radiates lushness with abundant flower and fiber embellishments and the soft texture of fine mesh.

Kay Rogers, Midland, Michigan

Supplies: Patterned papers, sticker, die-cut letters, number stickers, file folder, fibers (Basic Grey); metal washer (Making Memories); paper flowers (Prima); mesh (Magenta); textured cardstock (Bazzill); brads; stamping ink; circle punches

Showing Up to Your Life...

It can be tricky to combine large items in a layout, but Lauren found this commencement address so inspiring she just had to include it with her photos. Lauren's clever solution of using a transparency to overlay words in an inactive section of the photo lets everything shine.

Lauren McElroy, Wasilla, Alaska

Photos: Diana L. Bland of Hotshots Photography, Wasilla, Alaska

Supplies: Ribbon slides (Lasting Impressions); textured cardstock (Bazzill); ribbon (Maya Road); transparency; brads

Lauren

Somewhere between her first day of school and the last, Lauren became a young woman directing her own fate. For a scholarly layout decoration, Denise created a scroll from printed and embossed vellum. Inked, rolled and secured with double-sided adhesive, her completed diploma is accented with a painted filigree charm.

Denise Tucker, Versailles, Indiana

Photos: Jim Miller, Holton, Indiana

Supplies: Patterned papers (Rusty Pickle, Sandylion); metal key (Rusty Pickle); die-cut ruler (Daisy D's); velvet paper (Stampin' Up!); square and decorative brads (Making Memories); stamp numbers (All Night Media, Making Memories); metal letters (Karen Foster Design); metal charm (JewelCraft); label holder (Junkitz); sticker tag (Pebbles); label maker (Dymo); tassel (Stampendous!); trim (source unknown); twill (Creek Bank Creations); ribbon; string; stamping ink; distress ink; embossing powder; glossy and acrylic paint; vellum; foam spacers

Lisa

These spirited photos displayed so much of her daughter's carefree personality that Sharon chose them to adorn the title page of Lisa's graduation album. Sharon fashioned the materials for this page on a computer adding lighthearted commentary to photos and an inspirational quote to the horizontal black bar.

Sharon Whitehead, Vernon, British Columbia, Canada

Supplies: Textured cardstock (Bazzill); image-editing software (Adobe Photoshop)

Friends

Rebekah's layout pays tribute to friendships so perfect they may never come again. To calm the overpowering brightness of her photo's red gowns on bricks, Rebekah began by removing all color. The retouched photo draws out the faces and allows Rebekah to subtly reintroduce her school colors of black and red into the design using fun patterned papers.

Rebekah Robinson, Shelocta, Pennsylvania

Photo: Janice Burch, Elderton, Pennsylvania

Supplies: Patterned papers (DieCuts with a View, Pebbles); tag (Avery); metal-rimmed tag (Making Memories); die-cut letter (My Mind's Eye); letter stickers (Creative Imaginations); chalk (Deluxe Designs)

Great Expectations

The empty chairs of this computer-generated layout represent eighth-graders advancing into new adventures. To symbolize the contrast between old and new expectations, Tonya added a bright pink box to frame the black-and-white photos of her beautiful daughter, Shade.

Tonya Doughty, Wenatchee, Washington

Supplies: Patterned paper, typewriter accents (www.scrapgirls.com); distressed kraft cardstock (www.gauchogirl.com)

All You Need Is Love

Friends, family and loved ones are truly the stuff joy is made of. School pals to share laughter and play, siblings to torment, parents to depend on, aunts and uncles to look up to, and, of course, teen sweethearts to court and maybe even kiss when Mom and Dad aren't looking. The love expressed between teen youngsters and those closest to their hearts may turn up the blush-o-meter, but there is certainly no better way to capture emotion on scrapbook pages than to document these precious times.

Friend

This photo of Amberley and her three best friends captures their carefree natures and the close bond they have shared since preschool, memories she treasures as they separate to pursue their educations. Amberley's lighthearted layout highlights the fun of her photo with fresh colors and handcrafted canvas letters.

Amberley Stevens, London, Ontario, Canada

Photo: Samira Dean, London, Ontario, Canada

Supplies: Patterned papers (KI Memories, Rusty Pickle); textured cardstock (Bazzill); printed twill (Creative Impressions); letter stamps (Making Memories); label maker (Dymo); canvas fabric; brads

Friends Forever

It began with a shared love of riding, ripened with fun times, and deepened during the loss of Shelby's horse. Thirteen-year-old Emma treasures this genuine, close relationship and commemorates it in her layout about the importance of true friendships. Emma made matching accents by placing patterned paper under epoxy stickers.

Emma Laffoley, Riverview, New Brunswick, Canada

Photos: Kathy Thompson Laffoley, Riverview, New Brunswick, Canada

Supplies: Patterned papers (Basic Grey); epoxy stickers (Making Memories); design stamps (source unknown); textured cardstock (Bazzill); mini brads (Doodlebug Design)

Summer Camp 2005

These photos of kids leaving for summer church camp made Courtney realize how much she loves the excited faces of the kids. To insert that same exuberance into her layout, Courtney combines bright colors, buttons and a handcut paper edge accented with writing.

Courtney Walsh, Winnebago, Illinois

Supplies: Patterned paper (source unknown); buttons; stamping ink; decorative scissors

What Happened?

When Becky met them, Hope and Joy were tiny and they grew up before her eyes. Nevertheless, the little girls are still here, just bigger and more beautiful than ever before. For a fresh youthful look, Becky stitched frayed fabric to her page and blocked her title with tags.

Becky Novacek, Fremont, Nebraska

Supplies: Patterned papers (Chatterbox, Scenic Route Paper Co.); chipboard letters (Li'l Davis Designs); rub-on letters (Autumn Leaves); symbol stamp (source unknown); stamping ink; tags; fabric; rickrack; staples

FOOD FRIENDS

IT DOESN'T REALLY MATTER WHAT HANNAH AND AUBREE DO TOGETHER, THEY ACT GOOFY NO MATTER WHAT! SUMMER, 2004

FUN &

Food Friends & Fun

They may attend different schools but Hannah and Aubree meet as often as possible, and when they are together, watch out for goofy acts of fun. Kitty's design combines words and letters cut from alphabet paper and lively geometric prints to make a layout as giddy and unique as this friendship.

Kitty Foster, Snellville, Georgia

Supplies: Patterned papers (American Crafts); distress ink (Ranger); circle punch

Girls Friendship

Friends since the fifth grade, Kristy and Angel are so inseparable they are often mistaken for sisters. In her layout, Suzy replicates the coziness of a close friendship with a pastel palette that lends the page a soft, clean look. The flower and ribbon accents provide dimension to her page.

Suzy West, Fremont, California

Supplies: Patterned paper, tags (Basic Grey); chipboard letters, metal expression (Making Memories); ribbon (May Arts); acrylic paint; silk flower

girls friendship

Kristy and Angel have been friends since they were in the 5th grade. They are inseparable! People very often confuse them for sisters and even though they are not, they consider each other family.

There's nothing more important than girlfriends! The girls were sitting around one night and Jen and Megan shared that the "mean" girls had targeted them because they were tall. Well, the three older girls jumped right in offering support, sharing their similar stories and giving words of wisdom. Watching this conversation was so great. It's amazing what a few years of experience and maturity does. I'm so glad these girls have each other to get them through the turbulent teen years. What could've turned into a "Pity Party" ended up being a bonding experience that helped Jen and Megan feel truly empowered!

chat let's chat let's chat let's chat let's chat let's chat

Pity Party? Not!

Chocolate is good but girlfriends are better, especially when young high schoolers get the support and advice they need from those who have been there. Anabelle's pastel layout reflects the innocence of the girls, and her upbeat design integrates a computer-tinted photo with stamped and glittered embellishments.

Anabelle O'Malley for Paper Salon, Hockessin, Delaware

Supplies: Patterned paper, cardstock, stamping ink, flower and expression stamps (Paper Salon); letter stickers (Doodlebug Design); beads (Cousin Corp.); mesh (Magic Mesh); glitter; ribbon; transparency

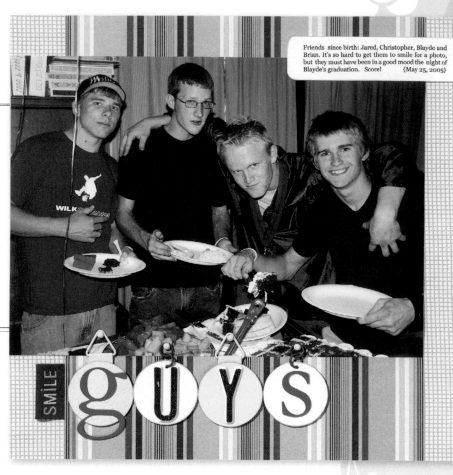

Smile Guys

It is not easy catching guys in a genuine smile, but on this night the mood was right and Kimberly scored a great shot. To celebrate her coup, Kimberly dominates her layout with a humongous look at the infectious grins and accents the photo with inked mesh and a dangling title.

Kimberly Kesti, Phoenix, Arizona

Supplies: Patterned paper, metal hangers (Daisy D's); mesh (Magic Mesh); metal letters (American Crafts); letter stickers (Sticker Studio); woven label (Scrapworks); jump rings (Junkitz); cardstock; brads; circle punch; stamping ink

What can I say about these guys? They are probably the craziest, goofiest, wildest dudes our family has ever met! You know what? We love it! These two have brought our family a lot of fun and laughter! Especially to Angel! They will sing, dance and do any kind of entertaining on a dare! They have even helped Angel do her chores!

We met the guys four years ago when Chad moved in across the street from my parents. Since then the boys and Angel have had many adventures together. They call me mom and come over all the time!

Rough rowdy

OH BOY
June 2005

Guys

Sometimes rowdy and entertaining, sometimes helpful and caring, these guys are proud to call each other friends. In her layout documenting their relationship, Suzy stresses masculinity through blue paper and a large unrefined chipboard title which includes a metal lid.

Suzy West, Fremont, California

Supplies: Patterned paper (Basic Grey); rub-on letters (Junkitz); chipboard letters (Heidi Swapp); metal lid (Design Originals); textured cardstock (Bazzill); stamping ink

3 Guys and Fred

Some of Fred's favorite memories come from performing with his group, and because Cheryl loved the group's animated style, she built melodic energy into her lively layout. To help her photos and journaling rise above the happy uproar, Cheryl neutralizes their colors, ensuring that they stand out.

Cheryl Manz, Paulding, Ohio

Supplies: Patterned paper (Scenic Route Paper Co.); letter stickers (American Crafts, Basic Grey); acrylic buckles (Junkitz); sticker definitions (Pebbles); tag (Avery); ribbon (May Arts); pen; stamping ink

Dream

Delight in the Day

E.F.Y., also known as Especially For Youth is an opportunity for me to hang out with people of my faith. There is scripture study and classes/activities and food. There are late-night discussions and dances. There is literally something to do all the time even if it's just chatting with friends on the lawn. Every year I go to the same place and see most of the same people. I always come home loaded with pictures, hilarious stories to tell, and new friends. I look forward to it every year and start thinking about it weeks in advance. It's one of my favorite activities every year. (2004)

EFY

Katie

Treasured times together FOREVER the best of friends

EFY

At the EFY (Especially for Youth) conference, Katie enjoys Scripture, dancing and hanging out with friends. She loves attending so much, her anticipation begins weeks in advance. Jennifer gave her layout a hip look by dramatically contrasting cool purple with hot orange—a trendy format that plays up her black-and-white photos.

Jennifer S. Gallacher, Savannah, Georgia

Supplies: Patterned paper (Chatterbox, KI Memories), punch-out expressions, rub-on expressions (C-Thru Ruler); rub-on letters, tile letters (Li'l Davis Designs); flower sequins (Doodlebug Design); ribbon (Offray); square punch (McGill); brads; cardstock

JOURNALING
When it comes to journaling, there are many methods you can employ to document the story or emotion behind the page. One way to pump up the word factor is to journal from the point-of-view of the subject. By writing in the subject's voice and employing his or her one-of-a-kind lingo (particularly funky teen dialect), you reflect the inner guy or girl and document the events or happenings of the day as seen from his or her unique perspective. You can ask your subject to draft the journaling that will accompany the photos on the page or present a series of questions to answer that describe how he or she felt or what made that event or experience special.

But what if your teen is shy and won't give you the scoop in his or her own words? There's a multitude of other creative journaling techniques that will add spice to your pages in the list to the right. So go ahead, write on!

- lists
- definition
- compare/contrast
- favorites
- five senses
- then & now
- turning point
- who, what, when, where, why & how

Bright as Flowers

Good friends are always there brightening your gloom like the flowers they bring, or so Kay's daughter realized while recovering from mono. Kay's layout complements the innocence and simplicity of her photo by placing it on a large block background which shifts from gloomy black to bright flower hues.

Kay Rogers, Midland, Michigan

Supplies: Patterned paper (KI Memories); printed transparency (Creative Imaginations); rub-on stitches (Doodlebug Design); flower punch-out (source unknown); textured cardstock (Bazzill); brads; tags; ribbon

I love this picture of the three of you. Em, you were recovering from mono, and the girls came by with a beautiful bouquet of flowers. I thought it was such a great testament to a wonderful friendship. You're lucky to have such great friends, girl!

Friends & Rivals

Keiren and Serge share a typical male bond based on common interests and spiced up with fun rivalries. In creating her layout, Colleen resourcefully paces the background to her own needs by adding paper strips to an already striped paper. Denim and metal accents complete the masculine look.

Colleen Macdonald, Winthrop, Western Australia, Australia

Supplies: Patterned papers, letter stickers (Li'l Davis Designs); metal-rimmed tags (Aussie Craft, Making Memories); buttons (Junkitz); rub-on letters (source unknown); ribbon (Li'l Davis Designs, May Arts)

Beautiful

Too young to date but ready to primp, Annette's daughter and her friends helped each other get their look together before their first semiformal dance. Annette's sassy layout speaks to the fun and flash of young fashion with a mischievous glitter created from combining paisley fabric and silver buckles.

Annette Lauts for Junkitz,
Saratoga Springs, Utah

Supplies: Patterned paper, buttons, acrylic buckle, printed twill, rub-on expression (Junkitz); silver buckles (Li'l Davis Designs); fabric; stamping ink

Although these girls have another year before they can date. They were excited to go to there semi formal 9th grade dance. Ausia went to find the perfect dress, she made a good choice she looked so beautiful. the day of the dance she and her friends went to get their hair done and then got ready all together. I don't know how the dance went (oh to be a fly on the wall) but they seemed to have a good time. after the school dance they went to the end of a church dance. Hands down they said the church dance was more fun. Next year these girls will be in high school and I'm sure we will see more formal dresses, beautiful hair do's, and perfectly polished finger nails But there will always be the memories of the first.

Boys Makeup FRIENDS School

Teen Connection

When Jill watches her son and his friends interact, she can't help but think that these bright, selfless and confident kids already rock the world. Jill brings teen style to her urban layout with a corrugated rub-on texture and uses a word puzzle title to give her design a youthful slant.

Jill Jackson-Mills, Roswell, Georgia

Supplies: Patterned papers (Creative Imaginations, KI Memories); letter stickers (Sticker Studio); chipboard letters (Li'l Davis Designs); buttons (Making Memories); rub-on texture (My Mind's Eye); textured cardstock (Bazzill); transparency; circle punch; stamping ink

TEEN ConnecTIOnN

I enjoy observing my son with his friends. It's so interesting to watch the dynamics of teenage friendships. They interact with joy, selflessness and genuine interest. They are fresh, cool, bright, athletic funny, and trendy. These young suburbanites exude strength and confidence. It is quite refreshing to see such a healthy union from this eclectic bunch of teens.

a whole day of

FRIENDS

hanging out

WHITNEY JOSH CHRIS JOSH SHERRELL

Friends

A whole day of hanging out together.
Talking, eating, laughing and
just enjoying each other's company.

Friends

Hanging out with friends is an essential piece of teen life, and Dana symbolizes the fun of youthful connecting in this energetic layout surging in funky color. She listed teen favorites on vertical journaling strips and heightened the excitement of her title design by matting the first letter and adding ribbon.

Dana Swords, Doswell, Virginia

Supplies: Patterned papers (Basic Grey); letter stamps (EK Success); stencil letters (source unknown); ribbon (Offray); cardstock; stamping ink; transparency

Just Like Family

From sports to video games, Trent and Nick do it together, and Nick visits the Tucker home so often he calls Denise "Mom." To infuse extreme depth into her design, Denise layered tiers of inked paper between foam spacers and reveals the dimension with indented rivets.

Denise Tucker, Versailles, Indiana

Supplies: Patterned papers (Basic Grey, Rusty Pickle); wooden letters (Walmart); rivets (Chatterbox); letter stamps (All Night Media); twill (Creek Bank Creations); cardstock; acrylic paint; chalk; stamping ink; foam spacers; staples

JUST LIKE

FAMILY

Families enjoy shared experiences, so I guess that's how you and Nick became such good friends. In this past year, you and Nick have participated in so many activities together, such as driver's education, basketball, video games, baseball, church youth group activities, and trips to professional sports games. Nick spends a lot of time in our home, and even calls me Mom. His pleasant disposition and ever-present smile make it easy for me to enjoy having a fourth son, and I consider him to be just like family!

A Fathers Treasure

The smile on her husband's face made Wanda realize that the joy they get from their girls is a genuine priceless treasure. For her funky computer-generated layout, Wanda converted her photo to black-and-white so that it would contrast with the bright red background.

Wanda Santiago-Cintron, Deerfield, Wisconsin

Supplies: Image-editing software (Microsoft Digital Image Pro 10); scrapbooking elements (Kit by Rhonna Farrer, www.twopeasinabucket.com)

Self Portrait

Their mother-daughter relationship is strong as steel and full of everyday joy. And whenever Evana worries about the challenges Kaitlyn will encounter in the future, this photo tells her they will grow through it together. Nic created a grown-up design featuring a cropped flower layered in stitched paper.

Nic Howard, Pukekone, South Auckland, New Zealand

Photo: Evana Willis, South Island, New Zealand

Supplies: Patterned paper (Scenic Route Paper Co.); flower trim (Making Memories); chipboard letters (Heidi Swapp); ribbon (Li'l Davis Designs); vellum

It is every mother's dream. To be able to stand eye to eye with our daughter, to laugh at the same jokes, to share the same sad times, to lean on each other, to share with each other, to talk about boys (ok..scary) and to be at one with each other.

Teen. It sounds so scary. It terrifies me. I have spent time telling you how hard times can be when you're a teen. I have tried to explain how sometimes we can feel so alone at this age. Our teen years can mould us and it is important to make the most of them and not have any expectations.

Education is the most important short-term goal with your future in mind. I have told you to care for yourself and never compromise your beliefs. I have stressed the importance of safe independence and boundaries. I often ask myself if I have forgotten something or if I have covered everything enough? When I am unsure I look at this picture. I see the happiness and the closeness that we have. I see that you are a teenager ...a young woman. I see a Mother & her daughter growing together. I see a priceless self-portrait.

MOM & DAD thank you

FOR

TAKING ME TO PRACTICE

HELPING WITH MY HOMEWORK

GIVING ME MY PRIVACY (SOMETIMES)

SUPPORTING ME WHEN I NEED IT

MAKING ME LUNCH

ACCEPTING MY FRIENDS

SHARING YOUR FAITH

WATCHING ME HIT MY FIRST HOME RUN

LAUGHING WITH ME

TEACHING ME HOW TO DRIVE

BEING REALLY GREAT PARENTS

Mom & Dad Thank You

Parenting is not always a thankless job; it sometimes leads to great relationships with remarkable people, your kids. To demonstrate how well David and his parents get along, Jessie created this heartfelt layout which she accented with washers for a distinctively masculine look.

Jessie Baldwin, Las Vegas, Nevada

Supplies: Patterned paper (KI Memories); letter stickers (Chatterbox); cardstock; washers

TIME CAPSULE

It's about time. We all know what time capsules are. Time capsules offer future generations a peek at what life was like "way back then." But you needn't bury items in the ground in a steel box to preserve precious memories to be remembered in the future. You can create a scrapbook time capsule by including pages about your teen's interests or favorites du jour in an album with sleeves left blank to grace future layouts documenting your teen's soon-to-be grown-up behaviors, habits, interests and desires.

Wondering what items to photograph or include on your teen's scrapbook time capsule?

- CD or DVD
- favorite magazine
- newspaper
- clothing or shoes
- list of top five goals
- list of top five worries
- name or photo of boyfriend/girlfriend
- popular newspaper or magazine ads
- favorite book
- matchbooks from favorite restaurant

Our Goofy Guys

Donna wanted Thanksgiving shots, but the longer she snapped the more spontaneous her guys became until she finally realized she was photographing their close, goofy bond. Donna highlighted her rollicking photo by enlarging and splitting it across two pages; the bottle caps and parent photo complete her look.

Donna Garza, Romeoville, Illinois

Supplies: Patterned paper (Junkitz); bottle caps, letter stickers (Mustard Moon); ribbon (May Arts); brads; cardstock

2 Teens

Sarah knows how different teens can be; her own two teens have opposite sizes, shapes, passions and temperaments. Sarah's jovial layout reflects the lighthearted fun of her situation with bright colors and playful acrylic accents. To attach her matching ribbons, Sarah punched holes in the page, then threaded and knotted the trims.

Sarah Moore, Hunterview, Singleton, New South Wales, Australia

Supplies: Patterned papers, acrylic circles, die-cut letters, ribbon (KI Memories); cardstock

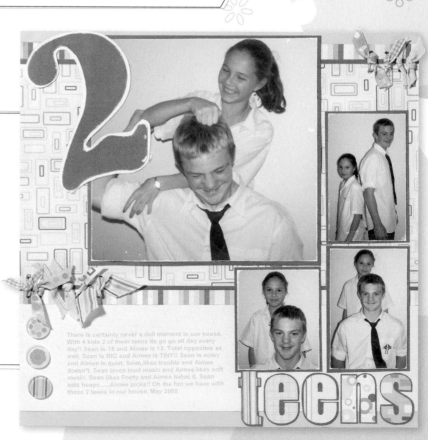

Brother

College-bound Kaleigh is close to her brother and took these photos to remind her of the laughter they have shared. Kaleigh designed her layout as a reminder to Seth of the importance of faith, and delivers her message through a variety of tag expressions attached with ribbon and safety pins.

Kaleigh Dees, Fayetteville, Arkansas

Supplies: Patterned papers, sticker expressions, tag expressions (Crossed Paths); large brad, safety pins (Making Memories); transparency definition (Daisy D's); textured cardstock (Bazzill); ribbon (Offray); stamping ink

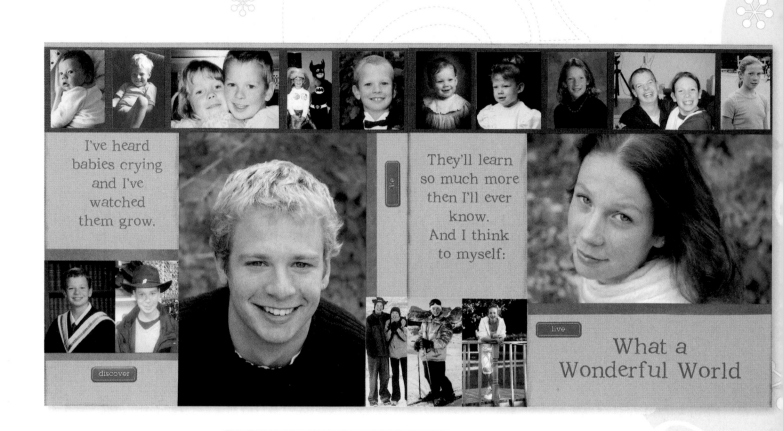

I've heard babies crying and I've watched them grow.

discover

They'll learn so much more then I'll ever know. And I think to myself:

tie

live

What a Wonderful World

What a Wonderful World

These song lyrics always remind Christine of two babies she has watched grow, her niece and nephew. To embellish her layout, Christine added many small photos of their fun times together and also injected her own version of the lyrics to proclaim how wonderful that world has been.

Christine Stoneman, Cumberland, Ontario, Canada

Lyrics: Bob Thiele and George David Weiss

Supplies: Word plaques (Making Memories); textured cardstock (Bazzill); distress ink (Ranger)

Sheryl and Me

When she was 15, Jennifer got a lovely baby niece. Who would have guessed that someday the baby would be 15 too? To document their now-close relationship, Jennifer took contemporary photos before a black backdrop and designed this informal stitched layout with handmade paper hinges for hidden journaling.

Jennifer Eschak, Edmonton, Alberta, Canada

Supplies: Patterned papers (EK Success); letter stickers (Provo Craft); metal-rimmed tag (Avery); textured cardstock (Bazzill); ribbon (Offray); eyelets

niece (nēs) n. 1 the daughter of one's brother or sister

LIFT

January 29, 2006

Sheryl

You were my first niece and I was so excited when you were born. I was 15 years old and I was so proud to be an aunt! I loved playing with you when you used to come for a sleepover at grandma and grandpa's house. Sometimes you would sleep with me and hog the bed! I would wake up with your little feet pressed into my back. I remember walking you to school on your first day of kindergarten with your mom and grandma. I can't believe you are in high school already! You still call me Auntie though and I love it. I am so proud of you. You are so smart, outgoing, ambitious and beautiful. I know you will be successful in anything you do! I love you!

Love Auntie Jen

Jennifer – 30 years

Sheryl – almost 15 years

S & K Together

There was always a special connection between Katie and her uncle, and now that she is older they hang out like friends. Samuel's "teen friendly" design combines patterns with torn, chalked and stamped textures for a playfully young look.

Samuel Cole, Oakdale, Minnesota

Supplies: Patterned papers (Carolee's Creations, Foofala, MOD-my own design); clock epoxy sticker, flower and circle punches (EK Success); paper tag (DMD); metal corners, metal-rimmed tag, epoxy circles, cardboard letters (Making Memories); metal expression (Colorbök); letter stamps, diamond stamp (Hero Arts); flower stamps (PSX Design, source unknown); spiral stamp (source unknown); ribbon (Heidi Swapp); chalk; cardstock; rickrack

Katie & I have always been so connected such good friends, so happy just to being out listen to music & enjoy each other. 6/05

Lucky to Have Each Other

Sarah and Ashleigh are cousins and best friends...what could be more perfect? To honor this delightful combination, Elizabeth designed this hip innovative layout. Its edgy look stems from offbeat color combinations, eclectic pattern mixtures and the youthful look of handwriting on lined school paper.

Elizabeth Cuzzacrea, Lockport, New York

Supplies: Patterned papers (KI Memories, Making Memories); paper flowers (Prima); rub-on and chipboard letters, rub-on hand (Li'l Davis Designs); rub-on flowers (Scrapworks); textured cardstock (Bazzill); photo corners (Heidi Swapp); brads (American Crafts); ribbon (Offray)

LUCKY to HAVE EACH Other

these two are so close. you would think they were sisters, but they are not. they're cousins. teen cousins. always giggling, telling secrets and having fun. lucky to be so close and always have someone there so lucky! Sarah & Ashleigh 06/19/05

Through the years Alex and Will have always been really close. They are just a few months apart in age and even though they only see each other a few times each year, their visits are always full of lots of catching up, laughter and tons of fun!

Colorful
COUSINS!
June 2005

Colorful Cousins

Since Alex and Will are both bright, animated people, it stands to reason they would be colorful friends. Kathy playfully altered her photos to complement her paper colors and theme, and then created a casual title by adding stickers and glaze to painted cardboard rectangles. Her stacked squares balance the letters.

Kathy Fesmire, Athens, Tennessee

Supplies: Patterned papers (Bo-Bunny Press); letter stickers (Bo-Bunny Press, Mustard Moon); square tiles (EK Success); date stamp (Making Memories); glaze (Duncan); ribbon (Offray); rickrack (Wrights); distress ink (Ranger); acrylic paint; staples

Please Not in Front of Mom

It is an age-old question with no clear answer: who is the most uncomfortable with open affection, the parent or the teen? Playing off the cool colors of her all-too-telling photo, Monique designed a contemporary layout using shapes and fonts for accents.

Monique McLean, Pelham, Alabama

Supplies: Patterned papers (Sassafras Lass); letter stickers (American Crafts, Sassafras Lass); label maker (Dymo); acrylic paint; cardstock

Grateful

Breanne can always count on Mike for support; even when she's stressing about fitting in at a party, he is there. Breanne's layout tells how grateful she is for their special friendship and includes a funky torn paper border to add flair to her design.

Breanne Crawford, Scotch Pines, New Jersey

Supplies: Patterned papers, circle punch-out (KI Memories); acrylic circles (Scrapworks); die-cut letters (QuicKutz); pen

YOU PUT THE BOOM BOOM INTO MY HEART

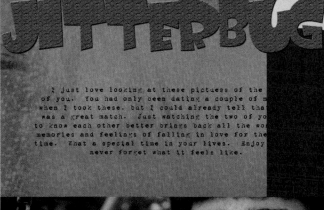

JITTERBUG

I just love looking at these pictures of the
of you. You had only been dating a couple of m
when I took these, but I could already tell that
was a great match. Just watching the two of yo
to know each other better brings back all the wo
memories and feelings of falling in love for the
time. What a special time in your lives. Enjoy
never forget what it feels like.

INTO MY BRAIN

You Put the Boom Boom Into My Heart

To Melinda, this lyric perfectly describes
the feeling of being young, newly in love
and happy just to be around each other.
Melinda's layout about her son and his first
serious girlfriend mimics the lighthearted
approach of the song with its bright geometrics and fun playful fonts.

Melinda Sabo, Hermiston, Oregon

Lyrics: George Michael

Supplies: Patterned paper, bottle caps, photo anchors,
effects (Cheeky Chic kit, www.scrapbook-bytes.com); vellum
tags (Digital Design Essentials by Gina Cabrera, www.dig
italdesignessentials.com); ribbon (All Tied Up by Jen Wilson,
www.scrapbook-bytes.com)

A BOY CALLED FRED

For most mothers...meeting their teenage daughter's first boyfriend is often a dreaded experience. When I discovered that Ashley was "going out" with the boy that she had a crush on in her 8th grade year, I was a little skeptical to say the least. Then she told me his name...FRED! I couldn't help but giggle...(it is a bit old fashioned after all.) and I was intrigued to meet the "boy named Fred.

We finally had the chance to meet Fred in the summer of 2003, when Ashley invited him over for a pizza dinner with our family. I was pleasantly surprised to find that Freddy (as we were introduced to him) was a very nice boy. He included our two younger daughters and played with each of them over the course of the night. This was surprising as most 14 year old boys would rather eat their sister's cooking than play with anyone under the age of 12!

Freddy was very polite throughout the evening, and at the end of the day, I knew that Ashley had found a "keeper" when before leaving, Freddy came right over to me, and said," Thank you very much for inviting me over. I had a great time, and thanks for dinner too!" WELL...Blow me over with a whistle!! I couldn't believe that this boy was the perfect match for our daughter...and over time, he has shown us again and again that he is really sincere, and cares deeply for Ashley. I know that they are young, and only time will tell whether they will end up together on their journey's through life, but I will always think of Ashley's first boyfriend and smile about...the boy named FRED!

LOVE

Fred – (Frĕd)
German: Peaceful ruler. Numerous royalty from Prussia, Germany, and the Holy Roman Empire have borne this name, including the thirteenth-century patron of the arts Frederick II of Germany, and the eighteenth-century Frederick II of Prussia who was known as *Friedrich der Grosse* (Frederick the Great). Familiar forms: Fred, Freddie, Freddy, Frici, Frits, Fritz

A Boy Called Fred

It was the boy's name that finally convinced Sue her daughter's first dating foray would be ok, and as it happens, Fred is as pleasant as his handle. Sue smeared acrylic paint over cardstock to produce a personalized matching background paper for her layout chronicling her story of parental adjustment.

Sue Street, Parksville, British Columbia, Canada

Supplies: Skeleton leaves (www.handmadepapers.com); textured cardstock (Bazzill); ribbon (Offray); vellum; transparency; brads; wire; acrylic paint; charms

LYRICS

Stuck in a rut trying to think of the perfect title or words for your layout? Song lyrics can provide the perfect inspiration to get your layouts rockin' to a fresh beat. It's easy to capture your teen's personality through song. Think of the qualities that mark his or her character or persona—is he or she an observer, a leader, a fiery soul, a hopeless romantic, an adventure-seeker? What collection of songs would make up the soundtrack of his or her life? Is there a song that puts him or her in a state of euphoria every time it's played on the radio? Or perhaps a ditty that marks a special event or occasion? Don't' forget that favorite quotes and poetry can also speak volumes to an emotion or feeling. Get your layouts totally in tune with these clever techniques that will keep you jammin' while you're scrappin'!

Having trouble remembering the exact words to that song or quote? Use these great Web sites for quick and easy reference:

- www.lyrics.com
- www.azlyrics.com
- www.lyricsworld.com
- www.sing365.com
- www.worldofquotes.com
- www.quotationspage.com
- www.quotegarden.com

Livin' the Good Life

intensity
B A S K E T B A L L

JUST AN ACTION SHOT OF YOU GOOFIN AROUND...PLAYING BASKET BALL WITH YOUR FATHER IN THE BACKYARD. NOW THAT YOU ARE OFF AT COLLEGE THE TIME YOU ARE HOME SEEMS MORE PRECIOUS THAN EVER.....APRIL 2005

Carefree, cool and livin' large, teens are the fortunate ones who can make their own luck and embrace the world with all its possibilities. Their days are filled with the adventure of sports and outdoor activities, the exhilaration of composing music and art, and the frenzy of hanging out with the crew at the mall or local gathering place. Documenting the dynamic life of a teen in scrapbooks will take you on a roller coaster ride of good times . . . ah, a teen's life for me!

Shutout

Imagine your first varsity start comes against a tough rival team and no one thinks you're ready. Nervous but determined, Ashley's brother met the challenge with a total shutout. In retelling this phenomenal story, Ashley's layout subdues all colors, sending our eyes to the amazing photo.

Ashley Hamman, Peru, Indiana

Photo: Tony Hare

Supplies: Patterned papers, stickers (Karen Foster Design); vellum expression (Memories Complete); letter stickers (Creative Imaginations); letter stamps (Hero Arts); label maker (Dymo); label holder (source unknown); metal framed expression (Scrapworks); wire mesh; tag; brads

Finding out I was getting the start just a few hours before the game was nerve wracking. A sophomore pitcher, who hasn't ever started a game before, to pitch against a rival team, and a pretty good one at that.

Almost no one had confidence in me pitching. Everyone thought we were going to lose, but we didn't and I threw a complete game shutout.

6-20-05

Chix with Stix

It is fast, it is furious, and they will not use their hands, only in girls lacrosse can you find chicks using these sticks. In this layout, Kelli created her own letter stamps by cutting traced die-cut letters out of fun foam, proving once again that chicks are also resourceful.

Kelli Noto, Centennial, Colorado

Supplies: Die-cut letters (QuicKutz); label maker (Dymo); die-cut lacrosse stick (Li'l Davis Designs); fun foam; stamping ink; cardstock

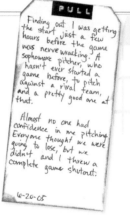

Freestyle

An athlete needs a remarkable heart, and here Elizabeth applauds the dedication which for years got her daughter Melanie up at dawn to practice and improve. In her layout, Elizabeth cunningly isolates Melanie in the group photo with a frame formed by the top of the letter "F."

Elizabeth Ruuska, Rensselaer, Indiana

Supplies: Patterned paper, acrylic letters (Junkitz); letter stickers (Mrs. Grossman's); metal-rimmed tags (American Tag Co.); vellum; acrylic paint

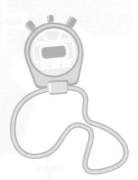

FREESTYLE

2005 is Melanie's 3rd year on Rensselar Summer Swim Team. You have to admire her dedication. She's up for practice at 7am every day.

And while she's not the fastest person on the team, she keeps improving. 6/4/05 Fountain @ Rensselar 50m free 42:31 6th place.

MORE THAN A GAME

This is so much more than a game to you. A chance to socialize, empathize, patronize and bond. Wear yourself out, stretch yourself thin, dig deep and play hard. A winning season no matter what the scorecard showed. 8th grade.

More Than a Game

Tonya hopes Shade's favorite memories of the season are of the joys of team bonding and her evolving self-confidence. As a reminder of the best part of competition, Tonya collaged action shots of Shade with several of her supporting her teammates, and then unified it all with a simple black border on this computer-generated layout.

Tonya Doughty, Wenatchee, Washington

Supplies: Monogram letter, wood number, slide mount (www.scrapgirls.com); kraft cardstock (www.gauchogirl.com)

Thousand Oaks H₂O Polo

Kelli's husband talks so eagerly about his water polo memories from high school that she just had to make a page featuring these action-packed photos. Amazingly, Kelli's layout nearly re-creates the texture of shadowed water through her use of mesh, patterned paper and distressed cardstock.

Kelli Lawlor, Norfolk, Virginia

Supplies: Patterned paper (Paper Fever); stencil letters (Autumn Leaves); label maker (Dymo); mesh (Scrapworks); circle tag, rub-on letters (Making Memories); metal word tag (Chronicle Books); epoxy sticker (Creative Imaginations); acrylic sticker (Li'l Davis Designs); textured cardstock (Bazzill); acrylic paint; brad

The Game

Every sport has a vocabulary, and in this layout Kimberly preserves the lingo of volleyball along with the memories of her daughter's season. To give her layout a high school look, Kimberly machine-stitched the large "P" to the page, creating a letter jacket effect.

Kimberly DeLong, Fremont, Michigan

Supplies: Patterned paper (Doodlebug Design); stickers (Karen Foster Design); acrylic letters (KI Memories); license plate (Sticker Studio); monogram letter (Scrapbook 101); chipboard letters (Li'l Davis Designs); ribbon (Offray); stamping ink; brads

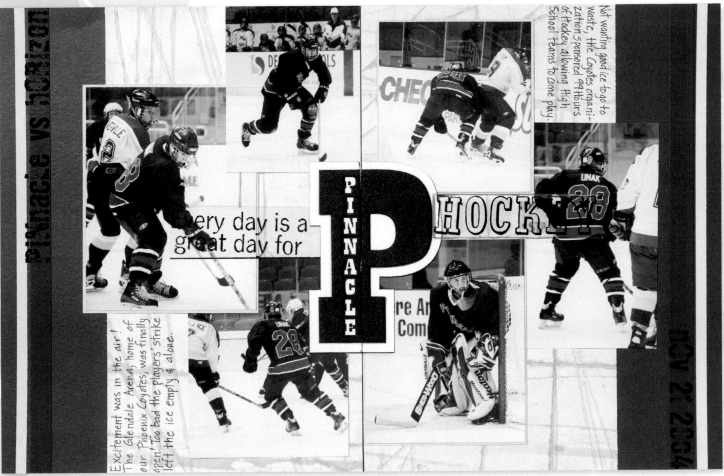

Every day is a great day for

Excitement was in the air! The Glendale Arena, home of our Phoenix Coyotes, was finally open! Too bad the players' strike left the ice empty & alone.

Not wanting good ice to go to waste, the Coyotes organization sponsored 99 hours of hockey allowing High School teams to come play.

NOV 21 2004

Pinnacle Hockey

Allison loves snapshots that illustrate the pace and intensity of hockey and wanted this layout to have the same sense of speed and motion. Her design includes lots of action-packed photos of her son and gains depth from her novel effect of applying adhesive to look like wet ice freshly carved with hockey skate blades.

Allison Landy, Phoenix, Arizona

Supplies: Patterned paper (Karen Foster Design); varsity letter (Paper Wizard); printed transparency (Daisy D's); epoxy sticker, rub-on letters (Creative Imaginations); dimensional adhesive (Ranger); cardstock

REACH for your GOALS

Brandon set some very high goals for himself at the beginning of his senior varsity basketball season (2001-2002). He achieved most of them. We had a great time in the stands cheering the team on. We're very proud of him.

Personal Stats
—6 feet, 6 inches tall
—center
—size 15 shoe

Game Stats
—averaged 17.4 points per game and 9.0 rebounds per game
—shot 61% from the floor
—had 45 steals and 38 assists
—took 15 charges
—had 14 double/doubles with points and rebounds
—held his opponent to 7.04 points per game

Goals Accomplished
—led the team to a District Title
—MVP on his team
—All-Conference first team WWAC East Division
—member of the Newaygo County TODAY 2002 Dream Team
—member of the 2001-2002 Muskegon Chronicle All-Area A-B Team
—Honorable Mention All State—Detroit Free Press

Job Well Done

Reach for Your Goals

Kimberly thought this photo exemplified Brandon's intensity on the court so she paired it with her son's goals and statistics to draw all the pieces of his season together. In her layout, Kimberly created an equally forceful title by assembling it from distinct fonts and accenting it with gold embossing powder.

Kimberly DeLong, Fremont, Michigan

Photo: Richard C. Wheater Sr. of Times Indicator Newspaper, Fremont, Michigan

Supplies: Photo border (Creative Imaginations); mesh paper (Magenta); sticker (Paper House Productions); stamping ink; embossing powder

Varsity Basketball

Content where she was, RyAnn learned a valuable life lesson when circumstances unexpectedly thrust her into a position that pushed her toward her real potential. Melodee's layout cleverly uses an epoxy square to spotlight RyAnn in the large photo.

Melodee Langworthy for Creative Imaginations, Rockford, Michigan

Supplies: Patterned paper, printed transparencies, letter stickers, resin charm, stickers, epoxy stickers (Creative Imaginations); rub-on basketball and jump ball (American Traditional Designs); textured cardstock (Bazzill)

RyAnn Spady
Freshmen Year 2004-2005
Imperial Lady Longhorn Basketball

by RyAnn:

During my freshmen year of basketball my game definitely changed from the beginning to the end. In VB season, I hardly played JV, and there were pretty much the same amount of girls in BB as there were in VB and so I really didn't figure that I'd play much JV either in BB. Then when I started quite a few of JV games, I was pretty excited and content with where I was. A few things happened with some of our older girls and they weren't able to play because of injuries which required our coach to drop down to the JV's and find someone who could fill the spot on the **varsity** team. When he gave me a chance, well...I was scared. Especially my first game, he put me in the 2nd quarter and I really thought that I made a big improvement from my JV game that night to the varsity **GAME**. The atmosphere is so different and I felt like a whole different basketball **player**. The intensity was unreal, I was glad that I wasn't too intimidated and stuck with it, and even scored 1 point. When **Coach** had me suit up again the next game and the next I was excited yet still a little scared. But in the end it all turned out for the best because I ended up starting in a game against one of the harder competition teams. Wow, that was one of the best memories I'll have during a BB game for quite a while. The best part of the season was...in the middle. That's when I started actually playing my level of competition and enjoying BB more. The hardest part was probably the intimidation of the older and better girls on my team. They were nice for the most part, but if you did one or two little things wrong then you had better watch out, they usually would get a little meaner on the **court**. But all in all my season was great and I'm looking forward to next season!!

Tackle Zone

Great sports shots are tricky, but Lisa got this photo of her son stopping the carry when the action came up in front of her. In her layout, Lisa created a unique accent by covering a stencil letter in paper and adding rub-on phrases, ribbon and a button.

Lisa Cornelius, Indianapolis, Indiana

Supplies: Patterned papers (Creative Imaginations, Mustard Moon); chipboard letters, metal buckle, metal hinges, rub-on expressions (Making Memories); epoxy expressions (Creative Imaginations); football button (Jesse James); textured cardstock (Bazzill); distress ink (Ranger); tag; ribbon; twill

WoW! What a TACKLE - It's amazing the teams could concentrate over the noise of the crowd. When the ball landed in the boys' hands it was like he didn't have to think he just ran, FAST!

Game On

Ribbons and bruises, intensity and hugs, Tiana is a superb blend of girly girl heart and competitor soul. Shawna's layout, a tribute to her daughter's complex nature, receives energy from the action of the small inset photos and the partial silhouette of the bat. To applaud Tiana's softer side, Shawna added pretty gingham ribbons.

Shawna Rendon, Memory Makers magazine

Supplies: Printed transparency (Creative Imaginations); chipboard letters (Li'l Davis Designs); baseball charms (Making Memories, Sticker Studio); letter stamps (FontWerks); ribbons (Hot Off The Press, May Arts); twill tape (Creek Bank Creations); brads; stamping ink

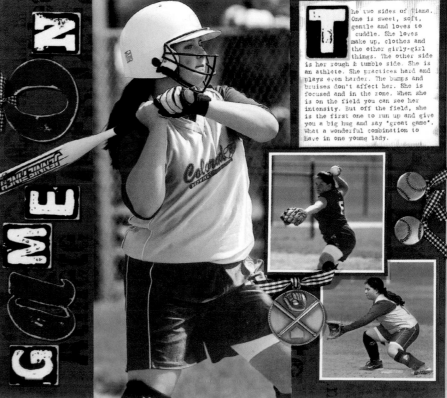

The two sides of Tiana. One is sweet, soft, gentle and loves to cuddle. She loves make up, clothes and the other girly-girl things. The other side is her rough & tumble side. She is an athlete. She practices hard and plays even harder. The bumps and bruises don't affect her. She is focused and in the zone. When she is on the field you can see her intensity. But off the field, she is the first one to run up and give you a big hug and say "great game". What a wonderful combination to have in one young lady.

Born to Snowboard

Living with snow several months a year is a blessing if you know how to use it. Shona's family loves snowboarding and in her layout describing the family's passion, she constructed an innovative quilt border made from paper expressions inked black and brown and then joined with stitching.

Shona Iverson, Saskatoon, Saskatchewan, Canada

Supplies: Patterned papers (Junkitz); cut-out expressions (Stamping Station); letter stamps (MoBe' Stamps!); dimensional M&M's sticker (EK Success); brads, floss (Karen Foster Design); distress inks (Ranger); stamping ink; embossing powder; twill

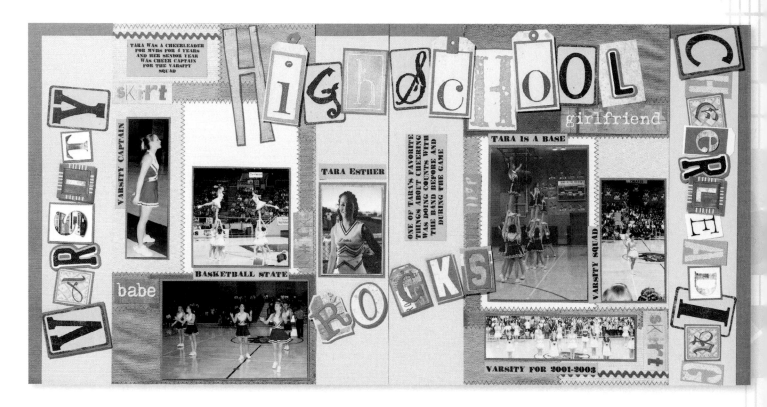

TARA WAS A CHEERLEADER FOR MVHS FOR 4 YEARS AND HER SENIOR YEAR WAS CHEER CAPTAIN FOR THE VARSITY SQUAD

HighSCHOOL CHEERLEADING

VARSITY

skirt

girlfriend

VARSITY CAPTAIN

TARA ESTHER

ONE OF TARA'S FAVORITE THINGS ABOUT CHEERING WAS DOING COUNTS WITH THE BAND BEFORE AND DURING THE GAME

TARA IS A BASE

BASKETBALL STATE

babe

ROCKS

VARSITY SQUAD

skirt

VARSITY FOR 2001-2003

Varsity High School Cheerleading

Whether on top or in the base, cheerleading is never boring so Michele wanted a knockout, teen-pleasing look for this layout about her daughter's squad. Michele's design creates plenty of sensation with a funky assortment of letters she collected from stickers, patterned paper and die cuts.

Michele Askeroth, Logandale, Nevada

Supplies: Patterned papers (Basic Grey, Daisy D's, Deluxe Designs, Karen Foster Design, K & Company, Provo Craft); letter stickers (Basic Grey, Magenta, Provo Craft, Scenic Route Paper Co., Sticker Studio); die-cut letters and tags (QuicKutz); wooden letters (Autumn Leaves); textured cardstock (Bazzill)

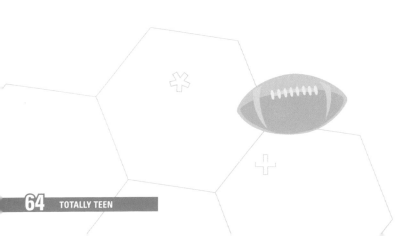

Potomac District 6/05
Falling Waters, WVA.

Kickin' Off Summer with Camp

inseparable!

Let the games begin!

Waiting for the bus to finally leave!

asking God for protection and His Blessing!

Kickin' Off Summer With Camp

It was very early morning but Deb's kids were so eager to get to camp her son started a pillow fight in the parking lot! Deb designed this computer-generated layout to resemble a collaged yearbook page, and to enhance the effect, included her own handwriting with a digital pen.

Deb Perry, Newport News, Virginia

Supplies: Image-editing software (Adobe Photoshop Creative Suite 2.0); patterned paper (Vintage Flavor kit by Ronna Penner, www.scrapbook-elements.com); digital pencil (Wacom Tablet)

COLOR CODING

How does your teen color their world? Is he or she drawn to vibrant bold colors or tend to bond with neutral earthy tones? A teen's favorite color can provide insight into what he or she is really like. You can reflect his or her personality, quirks and idiosyncrasies by utilizing colors on scrapbook pages that reflect the true inner guy or girl.

- Red = fun, funny and not afraid to be bold
- Yellow = optimistic and a good communicator
- Green = open, loyal and understanding
- Blue = creative, artistic and sensitive
- Brown = down-to-earth and trustworthy
- Black = serious and sophisticated

Dance Sing Play

Colt often takes his music outside to share with no one in particular or everyone within earshot. MaryJo loves her son's expressive confidence, and for the neighbors' sake, is thankful he's pretty good. To include more photos in her layout, MaryJo digitally created several mini collages of her extra shots.

MaryJo Regier, Memory Makers Books

Supplies: Patterned paper (Hot Off The Press); letter stickers (Mrs. Grossman's); die-cut guitars (Paper House Productions); note die cuts (source unknown); eyelets; sanding block; brads; thread

This year marked Derek's 14th birthday and the one thing he really wanted was an Apple "ipod"... a personal music player. With 20GB of storage, Derek can have about 500 songs at hand whenever he wants! He used his birthday money from Rick's parents to purchase the "ipod" and Rick and I gave him $50 to download some songs. Of all the goodies he received for his birthday, this one has already been so worth the $300 price tag! Derek uses it all the time... these photos were taken the afternoon we put up all the Halloween decorations and where was Derek? Up on the ladder... not hanging decorations, but listening to music on his "iopd"! Oh, well... what's a mother (or father) to do?

October 2004

ipod

Derek loves his personal music player and is lost in music even when he is supposed to be helping out, or so these photos show. Debi rocks her layout with dramatic color contrasts and a handcut title whose shape is subtly repeated in her playful circle and ribbon accent.

Debi Boler, Newport Beach, California

Supplies: Patterned paper (Chatterbox); rub-on letters (Junkitz); large and small circle conchos (Scrapworks); textured paper (FiberMark); ribbon (Junkitz, Making Memories); cardstock; corner rounder

Recording Time Gray Studios

When her son's band won time in a real recording studio, Janell gave Kyle a camera to record the experience with pictures, too. Janell put an electronic spin in her layout with geometric papers and a modernistic title font, then softened and unified the page with twine accents.

Janell Knudson, Littleton, Colorado

Supplies: Patterned paper, tag and circle punch-outs (KI Memories); miniature sheet music (www.printmini .com); note charm (Michaels); twine; fiber; cardstock

Raw Talent

A violin is far from hip to many teenage boys, but when Chris plays he makes it rock. Courtney's tribute to this gifted young musician from her church includes a rhythmic punched border fashioned from funky masculine prints. For interest, Courtney added a flower made of crumpled paper and a button.

Courtney Walsh, Winnebago, Illinois

Supplies: Patterned papers (Chatterbox); letter stickers (Making Memories, Mustard Moon); button (Junkitz); embroidery floss (DMC); cardstock; stamping ink; fabric; circle punches; pen

u rock

U Rock

Liz can only play one song on this guitar, but these photos gave Marta the right excuse to list the many things she both likes and loves about her daughter. Marta's layout gains an intimate feel by focusing on the close-up shots of hands and the large portrait of Liz.

Marta Gladden, Phoenix, Arizona

Supplies: Patterned paper, monogram letter (Basic Grey); letter stickers (American Crafts); index tab (Z-International); textured cardstock (Bazzill); distress ink (Ranger); mini brads (Making Memories)

I really "**like**" you Lizzy...
YOU ROCK!
All Moms "**love**" their children, but it is an added bonus when you really "**like**" them too!
*Your easy, uncomplicated style about everything **rocks**!
*The way you add energy to a room just by walking into it **rocks**!
*The fact that everyone is your friend **rocks**!
*Your crazy approach to fashion **rocks**!
*The way you sing in the shower **rocks**!
*Everything about you
ROCKS!

Lizzy | April 18, 2005

Mitchell, I am so happy you have found a way to express your creativity. I love to see you so interest and focused.

ART ART ART ART

A

IS FOR

Artistic

Create · imagine · desire

Art

A Is for Artistic

That look of creative concentration is real; Mitchell barely noticed his mom taking these photos. Beth's layout, an innovative tribute to her son's artistic nature, contains several of her own artsy creations including a printed label whose wet ink was smudged with paint, a hand-cut monogram and distressed, stamped paper.

Beth Sears, Quispamsis, New Brunswick, Canada

Supplies: Patterned papers, letter stickers (Basic Grey); rub-on expressions (Royal & Langnickel); stamp expressions (Hero Arts); label holder (source unknown); fiber (EK Success); textured cardstock (Bazzill); photo corners (Heidi Swapp); distress ink; acrylic paint; stamping ink; staples; pen

Wearable Art

With just a little time and a few markers, Melanie's ordinary garage sale shoes became an admired and personalized piece of art. Melanie's designs also embellish Elizabeth's layout which features close-up shots and large silhouetted feet.

Elizabeth Ruuska, Rensselaer, Indiana

Supplies: Patterned paper, printed ribbon (Junkitz); chipboard letters (Li'l Davis Designs); die-cut letters (QuicKutz)

Fashions Fade; Style is Eternal

WEAR

ABLE

ART

Grandma found the shoes at a garage sale. She bought them knowing they would fit someone eventually. The atmosphere became a mini-reenactment of Cinderella. Too big for Blythe, too little for Grace, Melanie was the recipient of the shoes.

But she already had plain white tennis shoes. She didn't need another pair. She needed FUN shoes. She needed COOL shoes. She needed to get busy!

Melanie grabbed her trusty box of Sharpie Markers and spent the afternoon personalizing her shoes. The results are obvious. She has a unique piece of wearable art. These one of a kind shoes are admired every time she wears them.

Focus

Marta often turns pictures into symbolic lessons, and these photos prompted her to think how life and photography often compare. To complement her theme, Marta's layout stays photo-oriented using black-and-white prints and minimal accents for a modern art flair.

Marta Gladden, Phoenix, Arizona

Supplies: Patterned papers (Basic Grey); chipboard letters (Making Memories); embroidery floss (DMC); textured cardstock (Bazzill); ribbon (Stampin' Up!); eyelet; brads; nailheads; tag; acrylic paint

I love these pictures of you taking pictures. They conjure up all kinds of metaphoric lessons I hope you will learn.

1. Focus on the beauty of your life
2. Remember balance and composition is everything
3. Life is lived in black and white
4. Don't forget to develop your film.

Sunrise til Sunset

Moved by the serenity of the water and reflecting sun, Patti snapped this shot of her daughter and dog after a hard day of play. Patti's layout uses a small inset framed photo to hint at the earlier fun and was inspired by the matching colors of the paper and photos.

Patti Hamil, Dawsonville, Georgia

Supplies: Patterned papers (Basic Grey); staples, metal frame, rub-on expressions, definition stickers (Making Memories); epoxy sticker (Creative Imaginations); paper bag (DMD); tag; ribbon; fiber; stamping ink

LAZY 1. not eager or willing to exert oneself 2. the state of idleness due to lack of desire 3. SLUGGISH

SUNRISE til SUNSET

WAKE BURNER

Sun Fun Hot

reminisce (rem'e-nis) to think, talk or write about remembered events, usually with fondness

RELAX 1. TO RELEASE TENSION 2. to rest from work 3. to be at ease 4. to release physical or mental pressures from oneself

Jenna and Patrick tubed all day and the whole time Speckles whined, barked and cried. Finally Patrick decided that she needed to ride. Needless to say, we didn't think she would but guess what? She actually tubed with them!!! The only problem was that she wanted to grab the rope and bite it whenever the boat stopped! May 2004

THIRTEEN

13

Not an adult, not a child.

Still plays with dolls, but thinks about boys.

Tall and lanky, slouches awkwardly when walking down the hall.

Wants to wear make up but can't apply it properly.

Wants to be a lawyer, ballerina, writer, book store owner, politician, entrepreneur, artist, opera singer, mother.

Self aware but not self confident.

Walks or rides a bike everywhere, but dreams of flying.

Thirteen

Here sits Jennifer in an adult swimsuit and burying herself in the sand. She's not a girl, not yet a woman, she's 13. This chic insightful layout from Jennifer's personal album uses dramatic colors and funky fonts to evoke the awkward imbalance of those in-between years.

Jennifer Lynn Moody, Lewisville, Texas

Photo: Roberta Moody, Fort Worth, Texas

Supplies: Patterned paper (Grassroots); rub-on letters (Autumn Leaves); textured cardstock (Bazzill); vellum

Star gazing

girls camp

Hiking the trail

Watching the Zion Movie on 6 story screen

ALOHA THEME

Flashlight: A small portable lamp usually powered by batteries. [syn: torch]

unity

This year was a Ward girls camp. We ended up going to Kolob Mtn. where the stake camp is, but we were there by our selves. We did different things than we normally do at stake camp. We just had so much fun and had a very spiritual time with the girls all pulling and working together so nicely.

• Campfire •

Girls Camp

Michele goes to girls camp with her church's youth group every summer, but this excursion was especially jampacked with activity. Hoping to include everything in one fun layout, Michele creatively utilized all page space and finally slipped the remaining photos into a funky pocket.

Michele Askeroth, Logandale, Nevada

Supplies: Patterned and velvet paper (SEI); punch-out letters (KI Memories); acrylic buckles (Junkitz); stickers (Karen Foster Design); tag stickers (Pebbles); flower eyelets (source unknown); ribbon (May Arts); textured cardstock (Bazzill); brads; tags; safety pin

Playing games

Came down a 100 ft. Cliff

Tubing down the Virgin River

Four wheeling

Survival game

• Campsite •

Hiking

PULL

We loved floating down the river on innertubes for a while, but then the sun would go behind a cloud, and Brrr. We thought, how long is 2 miles anyway, and by the time we got out, or the river we were freezing and glad it was over.

Crafting

Freedom

In a sea of bikes, he has his guts
In a sea of dads, he has his mom
In a sea of tools, he has his manual
In a sea of campers, he has his tent

No adversity will ever stop this boy
from the thrill of the race. What's
a mom to do but stand back (with a
first aid kit) and admire the tenacity.

Persevere

Although it is comfortable to blend in, what Beth most admires about her son is his ability to hang in there even when he sticks out from the pack. Beth affirms her admiration for Spencer in this computer-generated layout which gets a mechanical feel from the screw and chain accents.

Beth Ervin, Inver Grove Heights, Minnesota
Supplies: Scrapbooking software (www.cottagearts.net)

Fish

Becky's family has a long history of fishing, and Becky wanted to document how much Samantha enjoys it too. Her layout's graphic design and dramatic color contrasts help emphasize the photos depicting the old fishing adage: patience yields success.

Becky Thompson, Fruitland, Idaho
Supplies: Patterned papers, rub-on letters, punch-out letters (KI Memories); rub-on expression (Li'l Davis Designs); ribbon (Offray); corner rounder (Creative Memories); cardstock

Fishing genes run deep in the Thompson family, and Sam is no exception.

Just like her great-grandpa, grandpa & dad, Sam loves to drop a pole in the water.

Like any good fisherman, sometimes she even gets lucky enough to catch one.

Other times, it's a lot of hurry up and wait.

Last Days

To Evana, adolescence is a thrill ride hurtling breakneck down a mountain; and college departure is the shock of hitting the water below. To Kaitlyn, all of it is exhilarating! Nic's simple earth-toned design showcases the exciting photos illustrating her fun mother and daughter story.

Nic Howard, Pukekone, South Auckland, New Zealand

Photos: Evana Willis, South Island, New Zealand

Supplies: Patterned papers (Scenic Route Paper Co.); letter stickers (American Crafts); textured cardstock (Bazzill); ribbon (Doodle-bug Design); stamping ink

One of the hardest things about this awesome summer day in January 2005, was that it was one of the last days of your childhood. That is one of the last days before you leave me and step in adolescence. The Riwaka Flying Fox (or more like a flying gondola) was one of the things you had wanted to do the most before you left for college, so we set off to achieve your goal.

The day was a typical day with a gentle breeze blowing and the sun on our faces. You were excited at the prospect of hurtling down the side of a large hill at 128 kms per hour. I guess this is kind of ironic because as you stepped into the car with Dad, I realised at that second that this is how fast you are changing. I feel like your life is hurtling away, just like this ride you are about to take. As the car reaches the top of the hill and starts the decent it is then that I remember all of things that I have cherished about your childhood.

As you hit the water at the base of the ride a plume of spray is sent soaring into the sky. This is the second that I realise that you are a teenager. It does scare me, just as that wall of water did. I want to keep you safe and know that you are ok, but I guess this is how it feels to let go.

The look on your face as you climbed from the car was awesome. You were ready for anything. The exhilaration was so real. Looking back now I realise that we had to do something crazy to welcome your teens, we had to celebrate these last days.

CROP PARTY

Who's the most awesome artist on the planet? You! You know it and your teen knows it. He or she may joke that Mom is sick with scrapbooking fever, but deep down he or she marvels at your talent and creativity and cherishes the precious artwork infused with your deepest love and admiration. So why not share your passion and get your teen involved in the fun? Bring him or her to the craft table next time you crop, and allow him or her see firsthand the entire process of initial concept to finished design. You can share in the fun of shopping for patterned papers and embellishments and reminiscing at times gone by while organizing and selecting photos. In the process, you may get your youngster hooked on the hobby and have him or her well on the way to creating pages to be cherished forever.

Pampered

Just a few pampered indulgences can make all the difference between a mundane and glamorous lifestyle! With such a communicative snapshot to work with, Suzy muted the remainder of her layout design and let it speak out. She accents her page with only minimal paper elements and a monotone stamped title.

Suzy West for Paper Salon, Fremont, California

Supplies: Patterned papers, stamp flower (Paper Salon); letter stamps (Technique Tuesday); textured cardstock (Bazzill); stamping ink

Angel had such a great time shopping with her friends Kirsty and Ashley. They spent the day trying on clothes, checking out the cute guys, and looking for the perfect pair of sunglasses! When they were done they had a ton of bags, a ton of giggles, and as always a ton of fun memories! Oh and yes, they found the perfect pair of shades!

Girly Girls

Hang with friends, try a new look, check out the guys—a mall is there for so much more than shopping. Based on a grid of two-inch blocks designed and stamped by Suzy, this flirty layout accentuates her playful photos by including only simple flower accents.

Suzy West for Paper Salon, Fremont, California

Supplies: Patterned papers, stamp designs (Paper Salon); textured cardstock (Bazzill); stamping ink; silk flowers; brads

Mall Brats

Two mall-obsessed girls need elegant dresses for a dance—could their lives get any better? For this stylish feminine layout, Stacey stamped her own paper charms and added color, glitter and lacquer. Tied with ribbon and suspended from mesh, the charms create a chic, girlish border.

Stacey Stamitoles for Paper Salon, Sylvania, Ohio

Supplies: Patterned paper, card, design and expression stamps (Paper Salon); letter stickers (Bo-Bunny Press); glitter glue (Ranger); mesh (Magic Mesh); crystal lacquer (Sakura Hobby Craft); flower brad (Making Memories); watercolor pencils (Staedtler); stitched trim (Li'l Davis Designs); ribbon (May Arts, Offray); textured cardstock (Bazzill); stamping ink; corner rounder

Jamie and Stephanie are what you might call "mall brats"! They love to hang out at the mall and just take it all in. This particular day, they were in search of the perfect dress for their 8th grade dance. We went to several stores and they did manage to find a few dresses that they fell in love with. Westfield just completed a 117 MILLION dollar expansion to our local mall! I believe this would be referred to as "heaven" to a teenager! ☺ With a 16 theatre movie cinema, Coach Store, Pottery Barn and so many other stores....plus a new food court; they are never without something to do or look at!
—May 2005

CAUTION:

TEEN

IN THE HOUSE!

farewell to dollies, blankies & bows...
welcome to makeup, telephones & beaus!

This is my life.
It is my one
time to be me.
I want to
experience
every good thing

Caution: Teen in the House

When Kathy realized the room colors her niece chose matched her own way back when, she knew she had to do a layout about Katie's room. Kathy's block-style layout helps emphasize the busy photos, and her title letters were encapsulated in green and printed on white cardstock.

Kathy Montgomery, Rocklin, California

Photos: Lori Horton, Greenville, South Carolina

Supplies: Patterned papers (Colorbök, Doodlebug Design); monogram letter (Basic Grey); epoxy circles (EK Success); vellum quote (C-Thru Ruler); metal numbers (Making Memories); texture stamp (Uptown Design Company); circle punch (Family Treasures); textured cardstock, library pocket (Bazzill); floss (DMC); ribbon (Offray); acrylic paint

KATIE, IT'S STILL HARD FOR UNCLE ERIK AND I TO SEE THAT YOU'RE A TEENAGER ALREADY! SEEING THESE CANDIDS OF YOU AND YOUR GIRLFRIEND "HANGING OUT" IN YOUR FUNKY TEEN BEDROOM BRINGS BACK SUCH FOND MEMORIES OF MY OWN TEEN YEARS. YOU EVEN SEEM TO LOVE THE SAME COLORS I DID BACK THEN...THE PURPLES, GREENS, AND BLUES THAT ARE SO FUN TO COMBINE TOGETHER! AND WHEN I LOOK AT THE "TRINKETS" SCATTERED AROUND YOUR ROOM, I REMEMBER ALL THE FUN LITTLE BOXES THAT WERE FILLED WITH SPECIAL "TREASURES" & BEAUTY PRODUCTS...ALL THE FUN THINGS WE GIRLS NEED TO KEEP CLOSE TO US. I HOPE YOU ENJOY YOUR TEEN YEARS TO THE FULLEST...THEY GO BY ALL TOO QUICKLY!
XXOO Aunt

My in Room

on the cell

PHONE

WHITNEY

In My Room

When she's home Whitney is in her room doing what she likes best, and Amy's amusing layout illustrates just what this typical teen is up to. The layout's welcoming easy style originates from Amy's large readable letterings and a very organized quadrant design.

Amy Goldstein for Junkitz, Kent Lakes, New York

Supplies: Patterned papers, acrylic letters and circles, printed ribbon (Junkitz); tags (Making Memories); chipboard letters (Heidi Swapp, Making Memories); rub-on letters (Imagination Project); epoxy flowers (source unknown); fabric

Private time in her room is something most teens cherish and Whitney is no exception to that rule. She is constantly shoeing her sister out and shutting the door so she can gab on the PHONE, read magazines or just spend time with her favorite cat.

She and her FRIENDS spend hours on end just laying about discussing what they are going to do that evening or weekend, talking about boys, dates, cars and the latest concert they are planning to attend.

It is a RARITY to find her at home for more than a hour at any given time with her packed schedule of work and social events. So usually, her room is where she can be found if she is at home at ALL!

Sk8r Girl

Boarding is not just a passion Madison shares with her father; it is also her style, identity and means of remaining true to herself. To Madison, skating is the epitome of coolness. Edgy-looking photos inspired Alecia's artsy punk design which she developed through paint, metal hangers and hip digital elements.

Alecia Ackerman Grimm, Atlanta, Georgia

Supplies: Patterned papers (Basic Grey); fabric paper (Michael Miller Memories); picture hangers (Li'l Davis Designs); stencil letters (DieCuts with a View); flower, large letters, small letters (Reflections of Friends digital kit by Amy Jo Smith); distress ink (Ranger); acrylic paint; cord; brads; staples; cardstock

The Crazy Teen Scene

Tawsha is a girly girl, and Sherelle's layout shows us what that scene can mean. To give her layout a girly fuss and flair, Sherelle builds her background from round-edged paper strips which together create a scalloped edge border across the page top.

Sherelle Christensen for Creative Imaginations, Shelley, Idaho

Supplies: Patterned papers, stickers, epoxy stickers, letter stickers, resin bauble and buckles, printed transparency, envelope, label holder (Creative Imaginations); letter stamps (Rusty Pickle); rub-on expressions (Melissa Frances); rickrack; silk flower; ribbon; twill

Can You Hear Me Now?

Nyome was forever fighting connection problems as she tried to contact home during her trip to Puerto Rico. Inspired by a cell phone commercial, Wanda spreads humor throughout her bright and straight-forward computer-generated layout by keeping both the title and the photo large.

Wanda Santiago-Cintron, Deerfield, Wisconsin

Supplies: Image-editing software (Microsoft Digital Image Pro 10); scrapbooking elements (Tea Party kit by Shabby Princess, www.shabbyprincess.com)

While we were in Puerto Rico making sure she kept in touch with her son Nyome could be seen on the phone fighting with a bad connection. We would joke about it, Can you hear me now? At the time she didn't think it was funny. I wanted to make sure now that we laugh about it, to make it a happy memory. Nyome in Puerto Rico 2005

Dig the New Glasses?

Cody wanted photos of his new tinted lenses and Karen thought he looked so cool she just had to make a layout of them. To maintain a masculine mood in her layout, Karen handcrafted a distressed tag from an old file folder and denim.

Karen Moore, Tallahassee, Florida

Supplies: Patterned papers (Autumn Leaves, Creative Imaginations); mailbox letters (Making Memories); rub-on letters (Li'l Davis Designs); letter stamps (source unknown); textured cardstock (Bazzill); ribbon (May Arts, Michaels); fabric; eyelets; walnut ink

Thirteen

Kathy wanted to do a layout about Emma turning 13, and this delightfully lively paper suited where Emma was in her life right then—happy. Kathy contrasts the paper with a large black-and-white photo and used brads to create a bulleted list documenting her daughter's favorite things at this age.

Kathy Thompson Laffoley, Riverview, New Brunswick, Canada

Supplies: Patterned paper (KI Memories); letter stickers (Creative Imaginations); mini brads (Doodlebug Design)

Thirteen

right now, you are into:

- pink! (the colour)
- vanessa carlton and avril lavigne
- american idol and survivor
- astral you can't get in enough hours at the barn or on her back
- your friends
- shopping!

Jenna at 18

Patti thought this photo looked so totally Jenna that the definitions of her daughter's lifestyle just popped into her head when she saw it. Patti's monochrome design features descriptive word stickers on fun mini tags to let the world know what Jenna is about.

Patti Hamil, Dawsonville, Georgia

Supplies: Patterned paper, circle letters (SEI); number stickers (American Crafts); buckle, rub-on letters (Making Memories); epoxy words (Creative Imaginations); ribbons (Morex Corp., Offray); brads; vellum; stamping ink

The 10 10 Rule

Sleeping

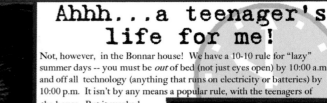

Ahhh...a teenager's life for me!

Not, however, in the Bonnar house! We have a 10-10 rule for "lazy" summer days -- you must be *out* of bed (not just eyes open) by 10:00 a.m. and off all technology (anything that runs on electricity or batteries) by 10:00 p.m. It isn't by any means a popular rule, with the teenagers of the house. But it worked out nicely for several reasons. I didn't have to be the bad guy in the morning. The alarm clock woke you up instead of me. It is much

Jammin'

better to have a teenager rustled out of bed by an alarm clock than "*the MOM.*" In the evenings, after 10:00 p.m., both of you would come and hang out with Dad and I. We'd play a little pool, chat about your day, watch a movie, or sometimes *nag* you about your chores... Of course, you didn't have much of a choice....because of the 10-10 rule -- the end result -- we spent some terrific family time together.

Computing

The 10 10 Rule

Knowing that everyone needs down time to recharge for what lies ahead, each summer Karen implements a unique rule which provides her teens space within healthy boundaries. The rule also allows Karen's layout to effortlessly flow into a graphic recap of her children's summer activities.

Karen Wilson-Bonnar, Pleasanton, California

Supplies: Image-editing software (Adobe Photoshop)

INSPIRATION

Looking for a little design inspiration or ideas for topics that are teen-related? Your own teen is probably inspiration enough, but if you find yourself needing the help from a muse, then turn to teen-trusted magazines that feature their lives up front and center. There's a wealth of teen mags on the market that offer unique and innovative ways to feature teens living life to the fullest. The following list is sampling of some great ones worth checking out:

- Breakaway
- Brio
- CosmoGIRL!
- Gumbo Teen Magazine
- Seventeen
- SG: Surf, Snow, Skate Girl
- Skateboarding
- Snowboarder
- Surfer
- Teen
- Teen Ink
- Teen People
- Teen Voices
- Twist

What I Like *About You*

Quirky, sassy, athletic, strong-willed, creative . . . every teen has his or her own set of characteristics that set him or her apart from the crowd. But whether your teen sets the trend or takes the road less traveled, no one can argue that the moments go by way too fast. So what better way to show your cosmically cool teen how much you love him or her than to put that kid with the killer smile front and center on a scrapbook page? Pay tribute to that quirky personality and unique identity on pages all about your unique teen.

Legally Teen

The years flew by and suddenly Scotty was 15, a young man with multiple talents and his dad's best friend. Martha treasures the many facets of her son and tells him so proudly in this layout which uses bottle caps and twist ties for an retro effect.

Martha Crowther, Salem, New Hampshire

Supplies: Patterned paper, sticker expressions, twill tape (Scenic Route Paper Co.); twist tie expressions (Pebbles); expression stamp (Limited Edition Rubberstamps); star sticker (7 Gypsies); envelope, bottle cap, chipboard letter (Li'l Davis Designs)

Scotty it is hard to believe I am the mother of a 15 year old son. The years have certainly flown by and it just seems like yesterday when I was changing your diapers and watching you run around in your underwear wearing cowboy boots and a cowboy hat.

I want you to know you have been a good son. You love being home with us and I love how much you and your dad spend time together. I will tell you a little secret. Your dad has told me often that you are his best friend and he is going to miss you when you leave for college. We both love you very much and are proud of your grades, your musical talents and your hockey talent. You're a special young man. The only thing I wish you would work on is being nicer to Brandon. Always know you hold a special place in our hearts. We love you.

Mom February 2005

Take My Breath Away

Sometimes a good hard look lends focus to what has been staring us in the face; as Suzy snapped this photo, her viewfinder revealed just how stunning her daughter had become. For her layout, Suzy played up her photo's casual edginess by distressing her paper and paint stamping her letters.

Suzy West, Fremont, California

Supplies: Patterned papers (KI Memories); letter stamps (Making Memories); metal buckle (Jo-Ann Stores); cardstock; acrylic paint

Take my BREATH away

While trying to snap this photo I had to stop and just look at you. Your beauty really took my breath away! I can't believe how much you've grown & how beautiful you've become.

Each year, when Emily has her pre-school candid pictures done, I try and get a decent shot of you, Josh, so that I can hang them side by side on the picture wall. This year, we went to Barber Park for that perfect shot. You actually cooperated too! That sure makes it easier to get the right picture. I plan to keep this going every year in the future instead of going for the annual school pictures. I think these are so much nicer! (just my humble opinion) ~Nov 2004

13 Yrs old

JOSH IN BLACK & WHITE

Josh in Black & White

Although Josh almost always frowns when he's photographed, each year Denise still tries for a picture to complement his sister's preschool portraits. Last year saw Josh's cooperation and Denise obtained outstanding shots. Her design features the photos in a nearly neutral setting conveying a strong sense of masculinity.

Denise Baker, Orlando, Florida

Supplies: Patterned paper, letter and number stickers (Imagination Project); letter stamps (Hero Arts); die-cut letters (QuicKutz); distress ink (Ranger); ribbon

Rated Teen

Based upon an existing, recognizable system, Angela has finally created a foolproof method to define adolescent behavior. How does your child rate? Inspired by the video game rating system and the colors of her photo, Angela uses a simple circle-based design to keep emphasis on her fun tongue-in-cheek message.

Angela Morris, Colorado Springs, Colorado

Supplies: Patterned papers (American Crafts, Daisy D's, My Mind's Eye); epoxy stickers (EK Success); letter stamps (Hero Arts); brads (Karen Foster Design, Making Memories); textured cardstock (Bazzill); stamping ink

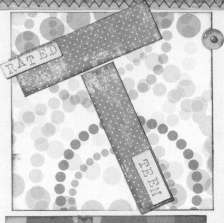

RATED FOR:

CRUDE HUMOR
BOTTOMLESS STOMACH
PRANKS
NOVELTY T-SHIRTS
VIDEO GAMES
SOCIAL ACTIVITY

YOUR VILLAGE CALLED...

Sweet-n-Sassy

Sue sees this photo as a perfect representation of her niece: sweet, mellow and a little bit sassy. Sue's appealingly fresh layout features flower accents cut from printed paper and a playful off-kilter frame.

Sue Fields, South Whitley, Indiana

Supplies: Patterned papers, stickers (Scrappy Cat); die cuts (My Mind s Eye); rub-on letters, letter stickers (Making Memories); fabric (Imagination Project)

My telephone is my LIFE!
My parents, my problem!
Boys - Boys - Boys! Talk to the Hand !!!

GROW
FOREVER YOUNG
I can't believe how fast you've grown. When we first met you were only 2, about the same age as Brandon right now. I was a selfish 18 year old going to college and dating your Dad. I didn't know what it meant to be a "mom". After a few years past and your Dad & I got married I started to realize how important family was and how important you were to me. I might just be your "Step-Mom", but I love you just the same. I worry about you, I care for you, and have many hopes and dreams for your future. Most of all I want you to be happy in life.. to be there for your little brother when he needs you whether that be in 10 years when he's 12 or in 30 when he's 32. I want you to faith in yourself and know you can be anything you want to be and I'll always be here for you no matter what. March 2005

Grow

Since they met 14 years ago, Sherry and Samantha's relationship has deeply grown. Sherry lovingly created this layout to tell her stepdaughter how much she cares about her and to relay her hope that Samantha and her baby brother will always stay close. Sherry paint stamped the title on a transparency for a crackled look.

Sherry Wright, West Branch, Michigan

Supplies: Patterned papers (Scenic Route Paper Co.); metal sign, letter stamps (Making Memories); textured cardstock (Bazzill); distress ink (Ranger); ribbon (Offray); acrylic paint; transparency

Thoughtful

The picture beckons, compelling us to discover the thoughts now dancing and fluttering in Lauren's dreams. To maximize the drawing power of her lovely, intriguing portrait, Renee features it large within her modest layout and balances it with a simple title accented with ribbon and a painted handcut letter.

Renee Hagler, Birmingham, Alabama

Supplies: Patterned paper (Imagination Project); die-cut letters (Sizzix); textured cardstock (Bazzill); ribbon (Morex Corp.); acrylic paint; staples

Dream

This luminous picture is so golden that Suzy's friends initially mistook it for a sepia print. Inspired by the photo's beautiful glow, Suzy's design evokes a sultry summer feeling through her use of color and the sunflower accent. Her title consists of letters cut from word paper and shaped into tiles.

Suzy West, Fremont, California

Supplies: Patterned papers (Scenic Route Paper Co.); flower brads (Making Memories); ribbon (May Arts); corner rounder (EK Success); silk flower; transparency; stamping ink

Delight in Your Youth

Sometimes her little brother is in a big hurry to grow up, so Lea treasures these photos revealing his young, innocent side; a part of Casey she always wants to remember. Lea's airy design incorporates a handcut title, stitching and a book of sisterly advice.

Lea Lawson, Missoula, Montana

Supplies: Patterned paper, die-cut frame, circle stickers, expression stickers, tags (SEI); metal letters (Making Memories); ribbon (May Arts, Offray); tag booklet (source unknown); distress ink (Ranger); fabric; button; stamping ink

Unmistakably Teen

Rebecca believes Leslie has turned totally teen, and she hilariously provides a symptom list to argue her point. In her layout, Rebecca creates more funky fun with bright colors and textured icons which identify each behavior.

Rebecca Cantu, Brownwood, Texas

Supplies: Patterned papers (American Crafts, KI Memories, 7 Gypsies); postage punch (McGill); letter stickers (American Crafts, Creative Imaginations, KI Memories); oval and square punch-outs, acrylic charm (KI Memories); stickers (Doodlebug Design, EK Success, Making Memories, Mary Englebreit); rub-on letters (KI Memories, Making Memories); letter stamps (Ma Vinci's Reliquary, PSX Design); leather and metal flowers, label holder (Making Memories)

A New Son

Karen was practicing her photography skills when she took this beautifully candid shot of her stepson, Cody, and the portrait became an opportunity to describe how much Cody enriches her life. Karen's simple design is intriguingly interesting due to perfect balance between the papers, photo and journaling block.

Karen Moore, Tallahassee, Florida

Supplies: Patterned papers (Basic Grey, Mustard Moon); decorative brad (Karen Foster Design)

slow down

you move too fast...

when emma was born, i heard this a lot: savour every minute, time goes by so fast. well, infancy with her was such a challenge, the colic was difficult and the fact that she was so wakeful and alert was challenging too. toddlerhood, minus a few mind-blowing tantrums, was fun and thus her childhood has unfolded. but all of a sudden, she turned thirteen. all of a sudden, time is moving at warp speed and i can barely keep up. she's such a great kid, she's so level headed and happy and so grounded, but life is moving too quickly for me. just like when she would do something adorable years ago that would make me smile, she now has the power to walk into the room and take my breath away: how did this happen? when did she start to look so much older, so together, and so beautiful in such a grown up way? when did what we talk about sometimes shift to such serious topics? how did she get to be this awesome human being whom i love spending time with and having in my life? i know i can't slow things down, i can't slow her down, so i am intentionally trying to savour it all, to make a point of really being in the moment, consciously weighing the answers i give her, the opinions i share. i am so proud of her, so happy to have her in my life, and given the option i probably wouldn't hold back time, but i am hoping these moments, these everyday happenings, are as important to her as they are to me. april 2005

laugh family joy together

Slow Down...

Kathy would have held back time to savor her daughter's childhood, but somehow time has warped ahead for her, or so it seems when Kathy sees grown-up Emma in these photos. In her layout, Kathy carefully arranges eye-catching stickers to create accents with a playfully retro look.

Kathy Thompson Laffoley, Riverview, New Brunswick, Canada

Lyrics: Paul Simon

Supplies: Patterned papers (KI Memories, Scrapworks); stickers (Scrapworks); rub-on letters and expressions (Making Memories); textured cardstock (Bazzill)

PHOTOGRAPHY
Composing strong photographs doesn't have to be rocket science if you follow a few basic principles. By working with the visual elements around you and allowing yourself to see creatively through the lens, you can compose pictures with fresh, unique perspectives. Here are a few basic tips to get you started:

- **GET CLOSE**
  Frame your subject as tightly as possible by getting in close and utilizing the zoom lens on your camera. Once you get close, compose your image and take a few test shots to be sure you have the perfect picture.

- **KEEP IT SIMPLE**
  Eliminate overpowering backgrounds by watching out for brightly colored objects, busy patterns and other detracting elements.

- **THE RULE OF THIRDS**
  In general, it's a good idea to not put your subject dead center in the frame. Instead, divide the frame into thirds, both horizontally and vertically, and position the elements along the intersections of the lines.

NOT A GIRL...

Katie is growing up so fast, I can't believe she is 15 already. She's such a beautiful young woman.

April 11
2005

NOT YET A WOMAN...

Not a Girl...Not Yet a Woman...

We see and feel a change of the soul as the child hangs back and the adult grows whole. Harley endearingly honors the progressing maturity of her sister, Katie, in this lovely digital layout. Her feminine design includes many layers, and the faded pastel tones help spotlight her photo.

Harley Rast, Florence, Alabama

Supplies: Scrapbooking elements (Kit from May Pole Mega Collection by Harley Rast, www.talinasdesigns.com)

Lindsae @ Fifteen Loves

Knowing teens encounter many ups and downs, Deb recorded Lindsae's likes, antics and many loves as a positive reminder of how beautiful she is inside and out. In her computer-generated layout, Deb created her own brushes to alter the kit's colors and textures into a funky bohemian look.

Deb Perry, Newport News, Virginia

Supplies: Image-editing software (Adobe Photoshop Creative Suite 2.0); patterned paper (Sweet Sprinkles kit by Kristie David, www.shabbyprincess.com)

Jesus
being with
family
pink
mini ipod
portrait pencil
drawing
chatting w/ friends
&blogging
room face & hair
makeovers

Lindsae @ fifteen
LOVES

LIFE @ 15

DAVID CARROLL
15 YEARS OLD

passing notes
in class
talking to girls

-HANGING OUT AFTER SCHOOL WITH FRIENDS

1. BASEBALL
2. CELL PHONE
3. LEARNING TO DRIVE
4. BRACES
5. IM (INSTANT MESSAGING)

TEAM PLAYER

whatever

ces Rules:
a pop, gum, candy,
on the cob, caramel
les, sticky candy
Brush between brackets
Floss regularly

COMPETITIVE

Sophomore

Life @ 15

Jessie wanted more than a tribute to this hip teen's interests—she wanted a layout reminiscent of David. In her layout, Jessie placed a colorful collage toward the center to enliven the overall design. The outer edges were then covered with scribbles and notes to instill her notebook effect.

Jessie Baldwin, Las Vegas, Nevada

Supplies: Textured paper (FiberMark); printed math transparency (Karen Foster Design); patterned paper (KI Memories); metallic paper (Magic Scraps); woven labels (Me & My Big Ideas); acrylic sentiment, washer (Making Memories); canvas expression (Li'l Davis Designs); circle stamps (FontWerks); number stamps (Ma Vinci's Reliquary); stamping ink

We got to chatting the other night, you and I Keiren, and mid conversation, it struck me how truly complex, intelligent and mature you are. As you approach your fourteenth birthday, I have been looking up at my little boy, looking for some childish reminders of the babe I used to hold and cuddle. While part of me is sad to realize that that little boy has only small traces left within you, I must say that I am proud of the young man you are turning into.

Hard to Fathom Your Depth

One day in the midst of conversation, Colleen realized how deep and complex Keiren's personality had become. To record how proud she is watching her son as he discovers his own emerging character, Colleen designed this thoughtful layout using painted cardstock squares and sticker letters for her title.

Colleen Macdonald, Winthrop, Western Australia, Australia

Supplies: Patterned papers, rub-on expressions, patterned letters (Li'l Davis Designs); letter stickers (K & Company); number stickers (Avery); artist trading card (Collections); metal tab (7 Gypsies); photo anchors (source unknown); acrylic paint; stamping ink; ribbon

WHOA Baby

WHOA, baby...STOP THE TRAIN! Who's looking so cool in her new shades? It seems like Brittany is totally transformed when she puts her new sunglasses on. Her whole HIP personality comes alive. She dons a tRENDy pea coat, knit scarf (wrapped just right), newsboy hat and leather gloves topped of with her "cooler THAN cool" shades. Now she's ready to head out the door and face the world! Brittany has always been a top to bottom girl. From the time she was little she made sure everything matched and that she was completely decked out head to toe. I guess some things never change! March, 2005

Whoa Baby

These pictures, which were shot after Sharon caught her daughter posing with her shades on, inspired this fun layout documenting Brittany's love for "decking out." Sharon's layout makes its own cooler-than-cool statement with flirty colors sewn on paper blocks and rhinestones.

Sharon Laakkonen, Superior, Wisconsin

Supplies: Patterned papers (Be Unique); chipboard letters (Li'l Davis Designs); letter stickers (Creative Imaginations); rhinestones (Mark Richards); staples (Making Memories); ribbon (May Arts); transparency

INTERVIEW

Teens can be a tricky bunch to decode. One day exuberant and excited, the next solemn and serious, they are forever adapting to each day's joys and challenges. If you're having trouble getting them to talk about their feelings, passions, pet peeves or even just a retelling of the day's events, use these questions to get them to open up and feed your creative fire with some fuel for documenting their personalities, quirks and other traits on scrapbook pages all about them.

- My best friend is…
- I currently have a crush on…
- My absolute favorite song is…
- My totally favorite outfit is…
- At school, I enjoy…
- The food I crave most is…
- If I could change one thing about myself it would be…
- My all-time favorite sport is…
- I crack up laughing when…
- People describe me as…

- I describe myself as…
- My favorite animal is…
- The color I'm most drawn to is…
- The goal I'm most focused on now is…
- I can't wait for the time when…
- My greatest joy in life is…
- My greatest fear in life is…
- My idea of a perfect date is…
- In five years I will be…
- I'm unique because…

Jenna

You will always be **BEAUTIFUL** **IN MY EYES....** *and that*

BEAUTY BEAUTY BEAUTY BEAUTY BEAUTY BEAUTY BEAUTY BEAUTY BEAUTY

BEAUTY *comes from* **WITHIN.**

Beauty Comes From Within

Colleen knew her niece was blossoming into a lovely young lady, but this photo in particular radiated Jenna's inner beauty and showed how Jenna was blooming from within. Colleen's layout also blossoms with chic fresh colors and a painted garden border.

Colleen Moses, Lake Junaluska, North Carolina

Supplies: Patterned papers (Autumn Leaves, Basic Grey); file folder, epoxy flower, printed transparency, rub-on letters (Autumn Leaves); letter stickers (Creative Memories); resin circle (EK Success); metal molding (Making Memories); monogram letter (My Mind's Eye); daisy clip art (Microsoft Picture It!); photo corners; brads; transparency; hairpin; acrylic paint

Jenna

I AM ALWAYS AMAZED BY YOU!

LIVING NEARLY 4 STATES APART HAS DEFINITELY MADE IT DIFFICULT FOR ME TO SHARE IN YOUR EVERYDAY LIFE...BUT THIS MUCH I KNOW FOR SURE, THAT IN SPITE OF OUR DISTANCE APART, I SEE YOU BLOSSOMING INTO A VERY BEAUTIFUL YOUNG LADY.

WHILE VISITING LAST SUMMER YOUR MOM AND I THOUGHT IT WOULD BE FUN TO HAVE AN IMPROMPTU PHOTO SHOOT AT UNCLE BRUCE'S HOUSE. AFTER SEEING ALL THE PHOTOS TAKEN OF YOU THAT AFTERNOON, I FELT THIS ONE PHOTO IN PARTICULAR EXPRESSED YOUR TRUE INNER BEAUTY.

I GUESS I REALIZED RIGHT THEN HOW MUCH YOU HAVE GROWN FROM THE LITTLE GIRL INTO A VERY SWEET, THOUGHTFUL AND LOVING TEENAGER WHO POSSESSES MORE MATURE CHARACTERISTICS OF COMPASSION, UNDERSTANDING AND SENSIBILITY THAT ARE BEYOND YOUR 16 YEARS OF AGE.

I AM SO PROUD OF THE PERSON YOU ARE BECOMING AND AS YOU CONTINUE TO GROW AND LEARN MORE, I HOPE THESE VERY SAME ATTRIBUTES WILL GUIDE YOU ALONG YOUR LIFE'S PATH.

IT'S EASY TO SEE THAT YOU ARE A PRETTY GIRL WHO LOVES WEARING MAKEUP AND DRESSING IN THE LATEST FASHION TRENDS. MY HOPE IS THAT YOU WILL ALWAYS REMEMBER THAT THE MOST IMPORTANT BEAUTY IS THAT WHICH COMES FROM WITHIN. IN MY EYES YOU WILL ALWAYS BE BEAUTIFUL FROM THE INSIDE OUT!

YOU RADIATE AND SHINE

Eric at Thirteen

Eric at Thirteen . . . Mercurial, recalcitrant, obstinate, independent, and maturing more and more with each day. When he was a toddler, he had to be dragged into bed every night, but as a teen, he has to be dragged out of bed every morning. Yes, Eric's favorite activity is sleeping. If we were to leave him alone on weekends, he'd probably be in bed until noon. Second favorite? Music. Eric has left behind Radio Disney and discovered Green Day. He burns his own mixes and downloads lyrics from the Internet. He still plays his trumpet, but he has also discovered the electric bass guitar. He likes to watch The Amazing Race, The Simpsons, Malcolm in the Middle, and CSI. He spends more time with his Gamecube than with books at this age, but he has just about memorized his favorite book, The Hitchhiker's Guide to the Galaxy. And girls? Yes, Eric has discovered girls . . .

Eric at Thirteen

This priceless expression is familiar to Kelli these days and representative of recent changes within her son. Kelli's layout gets its grungy look from paper patterns and photo distressing. Her creative number line was fashioned by masking and painting a transparency that reveals both the gray and the orange paper beneath.

Kelli Noto, Centennial, Colorado

Supplies: Patterned papers (Basic Grey); die-cut letters and numbers (QuickKutz); acrylic paint; transparency

You Can't Hide Beautiful

Raised on separate continents and together once a year, Jocelyn has still grown to appreciate the tremendous beauty within Michelle, her faraway cousin. Jocelyn's tranquil monotone design uses simple color swatches from vellum and satin to accent the intriguing beauty of her portrait.

Jocelyn Ou, Naperville, Illinois

Supplies: Patterned paper (Hot Off The Press); printed vellum (Paper Company); epoxy circle (Making Memories); ribbon; chalk

Michelle is one of my most favorite cousins and this is such a gorgeous picture that she took at one of those amazing photo studios in Taiwan when she was 13 or 14 years old. She is one of the strongest people I know and has dealt with so much. I was blown away when she told me about how Julie moved to New Zealand without ever getting to say good-bye except for leaving a note. Michelle is so independent and self-sufficient which are two qualities that I want to have. She's my "personality role model"—very sweet, caring, funny, helpful and of course completely brilliant! She's crazy, but can get down to business when necessary. Ever since I was two and we started going to Taiwan every other year (the years we don't go, they come over here), we've always had the best time with them. Michelle is always on my side—even when I'm wrong. She's the epitome of the meaning of "family" and I feel blessed to know her. I love this girl to death!

Beautiful (byōō'tĭ-fəl) *adj.* Having beauty in any of its forms; pleasing to the senses or the mind – **beau'ti-ful·ly** *adv.* –**beau'ti-ful-ness** *n.*
Synonyms: *beautiful, lovely, pretty, handsome, comely, fair*

It's almost too much for me to handle; my sweet tiny angel baby Courtney is 17 years old today. Yes yes I know, I've seen it coming for a long time and I've had 17 years to get used to the idea, but when I saw her today, so grown up, so beautiful and so independent in her new car, I have to admit I was just a little bit choked up.

I love talking to Courtney about her life now, she has a boyfriend, is popular at school, loves to shop for fun new fashions and is handling her parent's divorce well, even though it can't always be easy for her.

After some pictures we went to the mall, where Courtney, as always gave me some great fashion advice - she keeps me from becoming outdated, that's for sure! Then we met up with Reegan and Mike for lunch before heading back home. I wish they still wanted to come over to our place one weekend a month, but I guess at the same time I would be a little worried if they did still want to do that at this age.

I know it's a cliché, but no matter how old she gets, she'll always be a little angel baby to me!

May 8 th 2005

17

Christine has always been close to her niece and in these photos she sees both the little girl she has known for so long and the beautiful young lady Courtney has become. In her layout, Christine uses a butterfly charm to symbolize where Courtney is now—just starting to fly on her own.

Christine Stoneman, Cumberland, Ontario, Canada

Supplies: Patterned paper (Scenic Route Paper Co.); ribbon and charm kit (Multi Crafts); textured cardstock (Bazzill); date stamp (Making Memories); brad

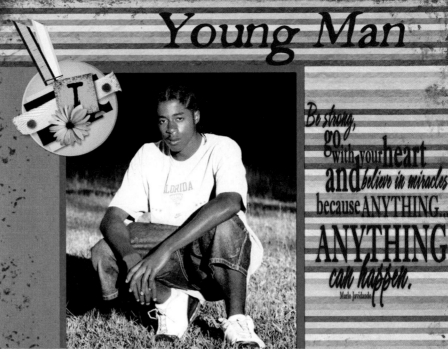

Young Man

It sneaked up on Michelle. Tyrone was working hard, preparing to graduate and making her proud, yet what a shock it was to realize he wasn't her baby any-more. Michelle's striking layout conveys her blessing on her son's passage toward adulthood with a large inspirational quote and an eye-catching tag.

Michelle Y. Thomas, Baldwin, Florida

Supplies: Scrapbooking elements (kit from Jen Wilson, www.scrapbook-bytes.com)

WILK TEAM

When I stop to think of all the things I admire about you, Christopher, your sense of entrepreneurship is one of the first that comes to mind. You became interested in skateboarding quite a few years ago and discovered that designing and ordering your own skateboards was definitely more economical than buying them from a shop. So, your small business, WILK Skateboards was born. Soon, you ordered t-shirts and sweatshirts for your friends. It was a small jump to hunt down a manufacturer of silicone bracelets and 50 white WILK skate bracelets are now for sale. Two skate videos were produced...the list goes on and on. You even bought an older Astro van, painted it orange and ordered a personalized plate! Every time someone told you "You can't do that", you found a way. I can't wait to see what the future holds for you. This week is your 18th birthday.

Love, Mom

Wilk Team

A few years ago, Christopher began designing and selling his own line of skateboards, skate videos and clothing. He even bought a company van, and, by the way, he is only 18. Kimberly's edgy "X & O" punk design contrasts white accents with the flashy colors of Christopher's company.

Kimberly Kesti, Phoenix, Arizona

Supplies: Patterned paper, buckle (Junkitz, KI Memories); chipboard letters (Li'l Davis Designs); target stamp (Hero Arts); stamping ink

First Crush

One night as Thane got into his wings and made lovey dovey faces while he ate, Suzy realized he was in the midst of a great infatuation. In her playful layout, Suzy keeps things simple, letting the graphic photos relate her humorous tale. Minimal accents and distressing help emphasize the pictures.

Suzy Plantamura, Laguna Niguel, California

Supplies: Patterned papers (Autumn Leaves); letter stickers (Autumn Leaves, Creative Imaginations); stitched trim (Li'l Davis Designs); rub-on and sticker expressions, epoxy sticker (7 Gypsies); stamping ink; brads; vellum

I thought when my boy turned 14, he would have his first crush. He does, but it is not at all what I thought it would be! He has fallen in love with Buffalo Wings. He can't get enough of them. He loves to go to dinner at Wing Nuts and we order them from Pizza Hut all the time. He eats the whole box full dipped in Ranch. He is seriously in love with his wings. Hopefully this is just a temporary crush! 05/05

love of my life   my heart skips a beat   first date   together forever

Laughter Is a Gift

Strange as it seems, Robin got this great photo of her co-worker's contagious laugh because a duck flew by just as she snapped the shot. Loving the photo, Robin used it to make this stitched and dotted zany layout as a present for Heather's birthday.

Robin Hohenstern, Brooklyn Park, Minnesota

Supplies: Patterned papers (Autumn Leaves); sticker quote (Cloud 9 Design); rub-on expression (Making Memories); label maker (Dymo); corrugated paper (DMD); ribbon (May Arts)

Daughters Life at 17

When Dianne came across her daughter's blog, she was so delightfully intrigued with Yvonne's self-description that she just had to transform it into a scrapbook page. To keep pace with the jampacked blog, Dianne included a mini album for additional space to record who Yvonne is at 17.

Dianne Hudson for Creative Imaginations, Tulsa, Oklahoma

Supplies: Patterned papers, negative transparencies (Creative Imaginations, KI Memories, Li'l Davis Designs); printed transparency (Daisy D's); stickers (EK Success, Paper Loft); letter stamps (Stampers Anonymous); metal letter, tags (Making Memories); conchos (Scrapworks); lapel pin (EK Success); label maker (Dymo); ribbon (Doodlebug Design); printed twill, bead letters, stencil letter, rub-on expressions (source unknown); tape measure; mailbox letters; jump rings

Daughter

beautiful

She is gentle; she is wild.
She's a riddle; she's a child.
She's a headache; she's an angel.
She's a girl!

ARYN'D

Daughter

Dianne took these spur-of-the-moment modeling shots after Aryn and her best friend tried out new hair and makeup techniques, something they do almost daily. Taking her cue from the outdoor photos, Dianne collaged a garden layout using pressed flowers, wood and torn paper for a natural feel.

Dianne Daigneault, Olympia, Washington

Lyrics: Oscar Hammerstein II

Supplies: Patterned papers (Karen Foster Design, Memories in the Making); die-cut flowers (Paper House Productions); dried flowers (Nature's Pressed); epoxy letters and numbers (K & Company); wooden frame (Li'l Davis Designs); decorative clip (EK Success); ephemera die cuts, vellum phrases, metal charms, epoxy pocket (source unknown); safety pin

The Name's Patrick
[Don't Touch The Hair]

Likes:
My Hair
XBox
Halo2
Star Wars
Final Fantasy
Sci-Fi
Hanging With Zach

Dislikes:
Cutting My Hair
Perky Cheerleader Types
Summer School
Cutting My Hair
My retainer

The Name's Patrick...

He won't look at the camera, he has hair in his face and he does not want to be messed with when playing his favorite XBox games...to Vanessa this is Patrick. To replicate the video games he loves to play, she used mesh as a stencil to stamp tiny silver holes sprinkled across the layout.

Vanessa Spady, Virginia Beach, Virginia

Photos: Jenna Beegle, Woodstock, Georgia

Supplies: Mesh (Magic Mesh); cardstock; stamping ink

Witty

Diana thinks her daughter's quick wit and ever-ready smile makes her an absolute delight to be around. In her layout, Diana uses embellishments with a variety of textures to reflect the variety of textures in Karee's personality.

Diana Furey, Malvern, Ohio

Supplies: Patterned paper (Design Originals, Imagination Project); 3-D expression, epoxy circles and letter stickers (K & Company); acrylic expressions (KI Memories); metal letters (Making Memories); wood letters and flower, chipboard expression (Li'l Davis Designs); acrylic letters (Junkitz); rivet (Chatterbox); flower punch (Marvy/Uchida); textured cardstock, chipboard squares (Bazzill); ribbon (May Arts); button, stencil letter (source unknown)

WITTY

You make me laugh! How many times a day do I absolutely crack up over your comments, your expressions, your body language? Remember on the plane when you did your "Claire" accent? How about "the toothpaste commercial smile; the "Kevin" jokes; "yo" Dad; "yeah... pantyhose; or, being in the single's group with Lindsay? I could go on and on with the funny things you say and do. It's a gift to be able to laugh and I believe it's an even greater gift to bring that laughter to others. You are just too funny. KareBear! Thanks for making me laugh!
Mom (January '05)

ASTONISHING

AFFECTION

you make ME

LAUGH

1 K 6

heart
so sweet
candy
kind
grace
sweeter

GET CRAFTY

Got a surplus of papers, stickers, embellishments or other scrapbook supplies and looking for a unique and crafty way to utilize them? Then look no further! Teens always seem to have a pocket or purse full of pens, pencils, key chains, chewing gum, cosmetics, and an embarrassment of other small items that seem to always appear underneath the sofa cushions. Use your scrapbook supplies to adorn crafty items and containers that will keep their personal effects in place. Or personalize a bulletin board or wall/door hanging that will make them appreciate your creative genious. Other fun ideas include:

- journal, diary or notebook
- mini-mirror for locker or room
- cosmetic case or basket for brushes, combs and scented lotions
- door hangers
- pencil cases or other mini storage cases
- bulletin boards or message boards
- book covers
- frames for photos, awards or certificates
- photo boxes

Beautiful...
Inside and Out

With college fast approaching for Emily, Kay wanted to tell her how much she admires her strong drive, high standards and the tremendous inner beauty she sees. Kay's layout features a stunning layered ripple effect, the result of several tiers of paper matting around each element in this lovely block design.

Kay Rogers, Midland, Michigan

Supplies: Patterned papers (KI Memories); paper flowers (Prima); mini brads (Doodlebug Design); ribbon (May Arts); cardstock; corner rounder

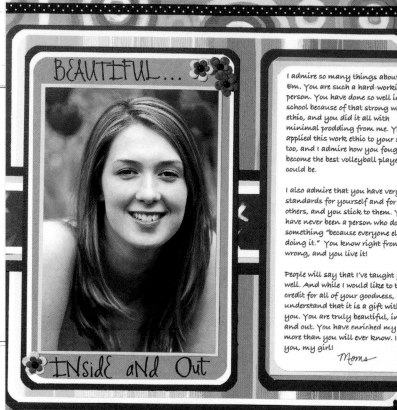

BEAUTIFUL...

INSidE aNd Out

I admire so many things about you, Em. You are such a hard-working person. You have done so well in school because of that strong work ethic, and you did it all with minimal prodding from me. You applied this work ethic to your sports too, and I admire how you fought to become the best volleyball player you could be.

I also admire that you have very high standards for yourself and for others, and you stick to them. You have never been a person who does something "because everyone else is doing it." You know right from wrong, and you live it!

People will say that I've taught you well. And while I would like to take credit for all of your goodness, I understand that it is a gift within you. You are truly beautiful, inside and out. You have enriched my life more than you will ever know. I love you, my girl!

Mom

on the verge

It's hard to comprehend that I've known you for 18 years. I've watched you grow from infancy to being on the verge of adulthood. Just a few more steps...and you're there.

On the Verge

As Chris walks those few steps to his diploma, he will cross a miraculous threshold leading out toward his future; he is on the verge of his own life. Jodi's buoyant layout celebrating her stepson uses form and color to step out of the box and, as you can see, it shapes up a little differently from other designs.

Jodi Amidei, Memory Makers Books

Photo: Kelli Noto, Centennial, Colorado

Supplies: Patterned papers (Arctic Frog); letter stickers (American Crafts); cardstock; foam spacers

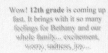

Wow! **12th grade** is coming up fast. It brings with it so many feelings for Bethany and our whole family... excitement, worry, sadness, joy...

We have home-schooled Bethany since Kindergarten. After doing this for 12 years, you would think we would have it all figured out. Not! 12th grade is uncharted territory for our family.

There are so many things to do this **last school year**:

- grad portraits
- SAT exam
- ACT exam
- portfolio presentation
- college inquiries
- college applications
- graduation preparations

There are so many feelings to work through. Have we done a good job **training** Bethany? Have we followed the right path with school choices? Have we prepared Bethany for her chosen **career**? Did we pass on our convictions and Christianity? Will her **roots** be deep and strong enough to make it "out there?"

Bethany is such a vital part of our **family**. We know we will be dealing with so much change in the next year and soon watching our first child leave the nest. It is exciting. It is scary. It is happening so fast! **This is it!**

THIS IS IT

The Final Lap

 2005-2006

This Is It

Sharon has always home-schooled Bethany, and now, as they approach senior year, Sharon is pondering graduation, Bethany's future, and all the training and roots she instilled along the way. Sharon lovingly preserves her thoughts in her layout, printing them on a transparency which she machine-stitched to the striped patterned paper background.

Sharon Laakkonen, Superior, Wisconsin

Supplies: Patterned papers (SEI); paper flower (Making Memories); flower punch (Emagination Crafts); letter stickers (Chatterbox); mini brads (Queen & Co.); transparency; ribbon

1   **7**   **11**   **33**

Additional Credits & Supplies

Models provided by Maximum Talent Agency, Denver, Colorado; Josiah, 13

PAGE 1

Brett

This striking layout does more than express Jodi's appreciation for the natural connection she has with her nephew; it is also a riotously fun spin through Jodi's abstract imagination. Unified through a repeating circle theme, Jodi's design grabs our attention through dramatic color contrasts and an original dotted bar motif.

Jodi Amidei, Memory Makers Books

Supplies: Patterned papers (Sassafras Lass); textured cardstock (Prism Papers); mini brads (Making Memories); circle cutter (Creative Memories); circle punches (EK Success)

PAGE 7

Sam Jammin'

Jodi's niece, Sam, is tappin' a cool beat at this outdoor family gathering. Machine-stitched patterned paper cut in circular shapes give the layout a smooth, free-flowing motion while floral papers coated with laquer add the perfect punch to the chipboard letter title.

Jodi Amidei, Memory Makers Books

Supplies: Patterned paper, 3-D sticker (Provo Craft); chipboard letters (Li'l Davis Designs); label maker (Dymo); crystal laquer (Plaid); textured cardstock (DMD); gel pen

PAGE 8
COOL TEEN PRODUCTS

Pretty n' Trendy

Patterned papers (American Traditional Designs, Carolee's Creations); cut-out flowers (Mc-

Call Pattern Company); stamps (DeNami Design Rubber Stamps); ribbon (Creative Impressions); beads (Me & My Big Ideas); paper clips, punch-outs (Carolee's Creations); bottle caps (Design Originals); twill ribbon, metal embellishments, stickers, vellum (American Traditional Designs)

PAGE 8
COOL TEEN PRODUCTS

Players of the Year

Patterned papers (Creative Imaginations, Design Originals); metal charms (American Traditional Designs, Sticker Studio); stickers (Creative Imaginations, Design Originals); self-adhesive labels (Creative Imaginations); stamps (Stampin' Up!)

PAGE 9
COOL TEEN PRODUCTS

Head of the Class

Patterned papers (Design Originals); stickers (EK Success); rub-on letters (Creative Imaginations); woven labels (Me & My Big Ideas); photo corners (Making Memories); word sticker (source unknown); photo frame (source unknown); cardstock

PAGE 9
COOL TEEN PRODUCTS

It's a Guy Thing

Patterned papers (Junkitz); word stickers (Karen Foster Design, Sassafras Lass); acrylic embellishments (Li'l Davis

Designs); stickers (Memories Complete, source unknown); sticker borders (Heidi Swapp); washers (Prym-Dritz); woven labels (Me & My Big Ideas); rubber embellishments (Sticker Studio); metal clips (Creative Impressions)

PAGE 11

In Full Bloom

Children are seeds we tenderly nurture, anticipating the day they blossom into caring and contributing adults; Denise's blooms budded so beautifully she placed them in a layout. To create the painted, boardlike appearance of her silhouetted flower, Denise used a decoupage coating and attached it with foam spacers.

Denise Tucker, Versailles, Indiana

Photos: Rebecca Eaton, Dillsboro, Indiana

Supplies: Patterned papers (Basic Grey, Design Originals); circle sticker, letter stickers, bottle caps (Design Originals); velvet paper (Stampin' Up!); mesh (Magic Mesh); wooden letters (Walmart); epoxy letters (Sulyn); letter stamps (All Night Media); decorative brads (Making Memories); textured cardstock (Bazzill); twill (Creek Bank Creations); decoupage medium (Plaid); clear transparency; stamping ink; embossing powder; foam spacers; acrylic paint

PAGE 33

Together

Some relationships are so easy that anything, at anytime is a great get-together. To celebrate the relaxed nature of this friendship, Dianne goes charmingly edgy by contrasting nervy colors with black-and-white photos and surrounding the focal shot in a burst of painted color.

Dianne Hudson for Creative Imaginations, Tulsa, Oklahoma

Supplies: Patterned paper, acrylic letters (KI Memories); clock transparency, label expressions and large rub-on letters, clock stickers, license plate, file folder, epoxy label holder (Creative Imaginations); stamp expression (EK Success); stitched borders (K & Company, Li'l Davis Designs); letter stencil (Autumn Leaves); clock hands (source unknown); label maker (Dymo); rickrack; brads; acrylic paint; cardstock

PAGE 55

High Intensity Basketball

Now that her son is off to college, Donna treasures the time he spends playing backyard ball at home. To give this computer-generated layout as much energy as the photo, Donna used a swirl brush effect and gave the picture an edgeless appearance by bleeding its colors into the background.

Donna Rafferty, Ashburnham, Massachusetts

Supplies: Background, edge effect (Kim Crother's Dirt Paper pack, www.scrapbook-bytes.com); swirl brush effect (Rhonna Farrer, www.twopeasinabucket.com)

PAGE 85

You R Younique

Every parent knows his or her child is a rare and special gift, but Dianne found over a dozen ways to say it. This truly feminine layout genteelly voices Dianne's opinion with pastels and fabric, and for additional texture she spot painted the backside of a transparency in pink.

55

85

105

105

Dianne Hudson for Creative Imaginations, Tulsa, Oklahoma

Supplies: Patterned papers, twill, acrylic plaque, buckle, stencil letter, sticker expressions, rub-on letters, printed transparency (Creative Imaginations); letter stamps (Ma Vinci's Reliquary); epoxy letter (source unknown); fabric corners (Making Memories); label maker (Dymo); acrylic charm (source unknown); fabric; acrylic paint

PAGE 105

Decorative Notebook

Jodi made this standard academic notebook go from drab to fab with pretty-in-pink papers and sparkling crystals. A buckle wrapped through pink twill gives it that extra dash of modern girl glitz.

Jodi Amidei, Memory Makers Books

Supplies: Patterned paper, buckle, twill (Creative Imaginations); crystals (EK Success, Mark Richards Enterprises, Mrs. Grossman's); stamping ink; notebook; pen

PAGE 105

Decorative Dry Erase Board

Torrey's sassy dry erase board has a lot to say when it comes to modern teen style. Funky lingo in the form of rub-on letters and acrylic charms shout cosmogirl cool in every way.

Torrey Scott, Thornton, Colorado

Supplies: Patterned paper, rub-on letters, acrylic charms, ribbon, buttons (Junkitz); white board; pen

Sources

The following companies manufacture products featured in this book. Please check your local retailers to find these materials, or go to a company's Web site for the latest product. In addition, we have made every attempt to properly credit the items mentioned in this book. We apologize to any company that we have listed incorrectly, and we would appreciate hearing from you.

7 Gypsies
(800) 588-6707
www.7gypsies.com

Adobe Systems Incorporated
(866) 766-2256
www.adobe.com

All My Memories
(888) 553-1998
www.allmymemories.com

All Night Media
(see Plaid Enterprises)

American Crafts
(801) 226-0747
www.americancrafts.com

American Tag Company
(800) 223-3956
www.americantag.net

American Traditional Designs®
(800) 448-6656
www.americantraditional.com

Anna Griffin, Inc.
(888) 817-8170
www.annagriffin.com

Arctic Frog
(479) 636-FROG
www.arcticfrog.com

Aussie Crafts no contact info

Autumn Leaves
(800) 588-6707
www.autumnleaves.com

Avery Dennison Corporation
(800) GO-AVERY
www.avery.com

Basic Grey™
(801) 451-6006
www.basicgrey.com

Bazzill Basics Paper
(480) 558-8557
www.bazzillbasics.com

Berwick Offray, LLC
(800) 344-5533
www.offray.com

Be Unique
(909) 927-5357
www.beuniqueinc.com

Bo-Bunny Press
(801) 771-4010
www.bobunny.com

Canson®, Inc.
(800) 628-9283
www.canson-us.com

Carolee's Creations®
(435) 563-1100
www.ccpaper.com

Chatterbox, Inc.
(208) 939-9133
www.chatterboxinc.com

Chronicle Books
(800) 722-6656
www.chroniclebooks.com

Cloud 9 Design
(763) 493-0990
www.cloud9design.biz

Collections no contact info

Colorbök™, Inc.
(800) 366-4660
www.colorbok.com

CottageArts.net™
www.cottagearts.net

Cousin Corporation of America, CCA®
(800) 366-2687
www.cousin.com

Creative Imaginations
(800) 942-6487
www.cigift.com

Creative Impressions Rubber Stamps, Inc.
(719) 596-4860
www.creativeimpressions.com

Creative Memories®
(800) 468-9335
www.creativememories.com

Creek Bank Creations, Inc.
(217) 427-5980
www.creekbankcreations.com

Crossed Paths™
(972) 393-3755
www.crossedpaths.net

Daisy D's Paper Company
(888) 601-8955
www.daisydspaper.com

Deluxe Designs
(480) 497-9005
www.deluxedesigns.com

DeNami Design Rubber Stamps
(253) 437-1626
www.denamidesign.com

Design Originals
(800) 877-0067
www.d-originals.com

DieCuts with a View™
(877) 221-6107
www.dcwv.com

DMC Corp.
(973) 589-0606
www.dmc.com

DMD Industries, Inc.
(800) 805-9890
www.dmdind.com

Doodlebug Design™ Inc.
(801) 966-9952
www.doodlebug.ws

Duncan Enterprises
(800) 782-6748
www.duncan-enterprises .com

Dymo
(800) 426-7827
www.dymo.com

EK Success™, Ltd.
(800) 524-1349
www.eksuccess.com

Emagination Crafts, Inc.
(866) 238-9770
www.emaginationcrafts.com

Family Treasures, Inc.®
www.familytreasures.com

FiberMark
(802) 257-0365
http://scrapbook.fibermark.com

FontWerks
(604) 942-3105
www.fontwerks.com

FoofaLa
(402) 330-3208
www.foofala.com

Gauchogirl Creative
www.gauchogirl.com

Grassroots™
(262) 695-6429
www.grassrootscreative.com

Great Balls of Fiber
(303) 697-5942
www.greatballsoffiber.com

Heidi Swapp/Advantus Corporation
(904) 482-0092
www.heidiswapp.com

Hero Arts® Rubber Stamps, Inc.
(800) 822-4376
www.heroarts.com

Hobby Lobby Stores, Inc.
www.hobbylobby.com

Hot Off The Press, Inc.
(800) 227-9595
www.paperpizazz.com

Imagination Project, Inc.
(513) 860-2711
www.imaginationproject.com

Jesse James & Co., Inc.
(610) 435-0201
www.jessejamesbutton.com

JewelCraft, LLC
(201) 223-0804
www.jewelcraft.biz

Jo-Ann Stores
(888) 739-4120
www.joann.com

Junkitz™
(732) 792-1108
www.junkitz.com

K & Company
(888) 244-2083
www.kandcompany.com

Kangaroo & Joey®, Inc.
(800) 646-8065
www.kangarooandjoey.com

Karen Foster Design
(801) 451-9779
www.karenfosterdesign.com

KI Memories
(972) 243-5595
www.kimemories.com

Lasting Impressions for Paper, Inc.
(801) 298-1979
www.lastingimpressions.com

Li'l Davis Designs
(949) 838-0344
www.lildavisdesigns.com

Limited Edition Rubberstamps
(650) 594-4242
www.limitededitionrs.com

Lucky Squirrel
(800) 462-4912
www.luckysquirrel.com

Magenta Rubber Stamps
(800) 565-5254
www.magentastyle.com

Magic Mesh
(651) 345-6374
www.magicmesh.com

Magic Scraps™
(972) 238-1838
www.magicscraps.com

Making Memories
(800) 286-5263
www.makingmemories.com

Mark Richards Enterprises, Inc.
(888) 901-0091
www.markrichardsusa.com

Marvy® Uchida/ Uchida of America, Corp.
(800) 541-5877
www.uchida.com

Mary Engelbreit Studios, Inc.
(800) 443-MARY
www.maryengelbreit.com

Ma Vinci's Reliquary
http://crafts.dm.net/mall/reliquary/

Maya Road, LLC
(214) 488-3279
www.mayaroad.com

May Arts
(800) 442-3950
www.mayarts.com

McCall Pattern Co., The
(212) 465-6849
www.mccall.com

McGill, Inc.
(800) 982-9884
www.mcgillinc.com

me & my BiG ideas®
(949) 883-2065
www.meandmybigideas.com

Melissa Frances/Heart & Home, Inc.
(905) 686-9031
www.melissafrances.com

Memories Complete™, LLC
(866) 966-6365
www.memoriescomplete.com

Memories in the Making/Leisure Arts
(800) 643-8030
www.leisurearts.com

Michael Miller Memories
(212) 704-0774
www.michaelmillermemories.com

Michaels® Arts & Crafts
(800) 642-4235
www.michaels.com

Microsoft Corporation
www.microsoft.com

MoBe' Stamps!
(925) 443-2101
www.mobestamps.com

MOD-my own design
(303) 641-8680
www.mod-myowndesign.com

Morex Corporation
(717) 852-7771
www.morexcorp.com

Mrs. Grossman's Paper Company
(800) 429-4549
www.mrsgrossmans.com

Multi Crafts- no contact info

Mustard Moon™
(408) 299-8542
www.mustardmoon.com

My Mind's Eye™, Inc.
(800) 665-5116
www.frame-ups.com

Nature's Pressed
(800) 850-2499
www.naturespressed.com

Paper Adventures®
(800) 525-3196
www.paperadventures.com

Paper Company, The/ANW Crestwood
(800) 525-3196
www.anwcrestwood.com

Paper Fever, Inc.
(800) 477-0902
www.paperfever.com

Paper House Productions®
(800) 255-7316
www.paperhouseproductions.com

Paper Loft
(866) 254-1961
www.paperloft.com

Paper Salon
(952) 445-6878
www.papersalon.com

Paper Wizard
(909) 627-1231
www.paperwiz.net

Pebbles, Inc.
(801) 224-1857
www.pebblesinc.com

Plaid Enterprises, Inc.
(800) 842-4197
www.plaidonline.com

Prima Marketing, Inc.
(909) 627-5532
www.mulberrypaperflowers.com

Prism™ Papers
(866) 902-1002
www.prismpapers.com

Provo Craft®
(888) 577-3545
www.provocraft.com

Prym-Dritz Corporation
www.dritz.com

PSX Design™
(800) 782-6748
www.psxdesign.com

Queen & Co.
(858) 485-5132
www.queenandcompany.com

QuicKutz, Inc.
(801) 765-1144
www.quickutz.com

Ranger Industries, Inc.
(800) 244-2211
www.rangerink.com

Royal® & Langnickel/Royal Brush Mfg.
(219) 660-4170
www.royalbrush.com

Rusty Pickle
(801) 746-1045
www.rustypickle.com

Sakura Hobby Craft
(310) 212-7878
www.sakuracraft.com

Sandylion Sticker Designs
(800) 387-4215
www.sandylion.com

Sassafras Lass
(801) 269-1331
www.sassafraslass.com

Scenic Route Paper Co.
(801) 785-0761
www.scenicroutepaper.com

Scrapbook 101- no contact info

Scrappy Cat™, LLC
(440) 234-4850
www.scrappycatcreations.com

Scrapworks, LLC
(801) 363-1010
www.scrapworks.com

SEI, Inc.
(800) 333-3279
www.shopsei.com

Sizzix®
(866) 742-4447
www.sizzix.com

Staedtler®, Inc.
(800) 927-7723
www.staedtler.us

Stampendous!®
(800) 869-0474
www.stampendous.com

Stampers Anonymous/The Creative Block
(888) 326-0012
www.stampersanonymous.com

Stampin' Up!®
(800) 782-6787
www.stampinup.com

Stamping Station™
(801) 444-3828
www.stampingstation.com

Sticker Studio™
(208) 322-2465
www.stickerstudio.com

Sulyn Industries, Inc.
(800) 257-8596
www.sulyn.com

Technique Tuesday, LLC
(503) 644-4073
www.techniquetuesday.com

Uptown Design Company™, The
(800) 888-3212
www.uptowndesign.com

Wal-Mart Stores, Inc.
(800) WALMART
www.walmart.com

Wordsworth
(719) 282-3495
www.wordsworthstamps.com

Wrights® Ribbon Accents
(877) 597-4448
www.wrights.com

Z-International, Inc.
www.zintl.com

Index

Learn more with these fine titles from Memory Makers Books!

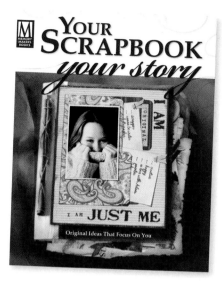

All Kids Scrapbook Pages
ISBN-13: 978-1-892127-63-1,
ISBN-10: 1-892127-63-6,
paperback, 112 pgs., #33440

Scrapbooking Family Memories
ISBN-13: 978-1-892127-59-4,
ISBN-10: 1-892127-59-8,
paperback, 128 pgs., #33439

Your Scrapbook, Your Story
ISBN-13: 978-1-892127-60-0,
ISBN-10: 1-892127-60-1,
paperback, 112 pgs., #33437

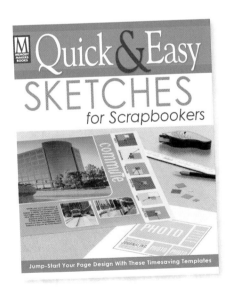

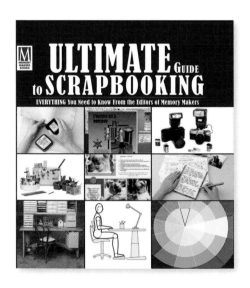

Quick & Easy Sketches for Scrapbookers
ISBN-13: 978-1-892127-64-8,
ISBN-10: 1-892127-64-4,
paperback, 96 pgs., #33436

Memory Makers Ultimate Guide to Scrapbooking
ISBN-13: 978-1-892127-65-5,
ISBN-10: 1-892127-65-2,
paperback, 224 pgs., #33438

All Men Scrapbook Pages
ISBN-13: 978-1-892127-67-9,
ISBN-10: 1-892127-67-9,
paperback, 112 pgs., #33441

These books and other fine Memory Makers Books titles are available from your local art or craft retailer, bookstore or online supplier. Please see page 2 of this book for contact information for Canada, Australia, the U.K. and Europe.